MENTALBALL

Also by Richard Crowley
and co-author
Joyce Mills

Therapeutic Metaphors for Children and the Child Within

Cartoon Magic

Sammy the Elephant & Mr. Camel

Fred Flintstone
Fred Protects the Vegetables

MENTALBALL™

BEAT
YOUR
INVISIBLE
OPPONENT
AT ITS OWN GAME

Dr. Richard Crowley
CREATOR OF THE CROWLEY METHOD™

Cahill House Publishing Company
www.cahillhousepublishing.com

Cover *Baseball Player* metal sculpture by artist Bill Arms. His life-size sculptures can be found at www.collectorsguide.com/ts/g372.html. His studio telephone number is 505-758-3039.

Cover concept by Richard Crowley

Cover graphics by Alponso Ramirez at CMG Industries www.cgm.la

Published by Cahill House Publishing Company
Los Angeles
www.cahillhousepublishing.com
2701 W. Alameda Ste 200
Burbank, California 91505
818-563-1449

ISBN: 0-9778566-2-3

Library of Congress Control Number: 2006901521

If not available at your local bookstore, this book may be ordered from www.sportsmaker.com or 2701 W. Alameda Ste 200
Burbank, California 91505
818-563-1449

DEDICATED to ROLAND HEMOND

Relentless in helping others achieve their dreams.
A gentleman in every sense of the word.
Beloved and admired by baseball.
An inspiration to all.
One of a kind.
A friend.

TABLE OF CONTENTS

Acknowledgements ……………………………………………………....vii

Foreword by Steve Blass ………………………………………………....ix

Foreword by Shawn Green …………………………………………........xi

Who Can Benefit from This Book ………………………………….....xiii

Introduction: It's Your Dream ……………………………………….1

Chapter 1: The Inexplicable ……………………………………….3

Chapter 2: Poster Boy for the Inexplicable ……………………….9

Chapter 3: Your Invisible Opponent ……………………………....15

Chapter 4: Unmasking Your Invisible Opponent ………………….21

Chapter 5: The Crowley Method and Mentalball ………………….26

Chapter 6: Imagination ……………………………………………….31

Chapter 7: Symbolic Images ……………………………………….37

Chapter 8: Visualization ...…………………………………………….40

Chapter 9: Remove the Fear Live the Dream ……………………….45

Chapter 10: Body Patterns on the Mound and at the Plate …………..53

Chapter 11: Conspiracy of Silence 59

Chapter 12: Remove the Clutter Quiet You Mind 65

Chapter 13: Judgment VS Compassion 73

Chapter 14: Full Blown Slump 76

Chapter 15: Dump Your Slump 81

Chapter 16: Well-Meaning Advice May Miss Its Target 84

Chapter 17: Target the Invisible Opponent Not the Mechanics 89

Chapter 18: Don't Lose Your Current Position 94

Chapter 19: Wohlers Finds the Strike Zone 99

ANATOMY OF THE DISCONNECT

Chapter 20: Point of Entry of the Disconnect 104

Chapter 21: No One Is Immune from the Disconnect 109

Chapter 22: The Disconnect of Players' Arms 115

Chapter 23: The Disconnect Behind the Plate 122

Chapter 24: The Disconnect at the Plate 126

Chapter 25: The Disconnect on the Mound 130

Chapter 26: The Disconnect with Fielding 133

Chapter 27: The Disconnect in the Infield 136

Chapter 28: The Disconnect in the Outfield 141

Chapter 29: The Disconnect Following Surgery 146

Chapter 30: The Disconnect Following an Injury 150

The End. Or Rather, Just the Beginning 154

Appendix A: Self-Assessment Survey: 100 Challenges Players Can Conquer 155

Appendix B: Completion of Three Players' Stories 159

Biographical Sketch 167

ACKNOWLEDGEMENTS

I wish to express my sincere gratitude to the athletes, clients and friends whose rich imaginations guided me to discover and learn about another world within our psyches containing the source of healing for overcoming life's obstacles.

I am grateful to others over the years whose influence and suggestions culminated in the completion of this book. They include my mentor Dr. Steve Heller, the seminal ideas of Carl G. Jung and Dr. Milton H. Erickson, and the innovative ideas and contributions of Dr. Joyce C. Mills with whom I co-wrote books and articles and lectured internationally. The contributions of Kilton Stuart and his widow, Clara Stuart Flagg, were invaluable in this process.

This book would never have been completed without the constant feedback, revisions and editorial skills of my brother John Paul. Equally responsible for the book's flow and outcome is Gail Sebern. Her editorial suggestions and vision taught me that less is better. Brian Walton's editorial and grammatical ideas saved me face as a novice in the ways of writing about baseball matters. Jeanne De Vivier Brown's expert line editing added the finishing touches. And Vince Kubilus' computer wizardry in the eleventh hour that saved the day.

Countless sports writers and reporters supported me by allowing me to use their articles to underscore my work. Contributions from Ken McLeod, Marion Woodman and the Institute of Noetic Science Review were greatly appreciated.

Taos artist and sports sculpturist, Bill Arms, was kind enough to allow the use of his life-size metal sculpture of a baseball pitcher for the cover. Suggestions from graphic artists Brian Sebern, Tim Hungerford and Alfonso Ramirez were invaluable for the book cover as well.

I am indebted to Mike Clancy and also Trish Harty, editor and co-owner of the *Irish American* magazine. In 1983 Mike encouraged me to contact former Los Angeles Dodgers second baseman Steve Sax. In 1998 it was Trish who was instrumental in my seeking former Atlanta Braves closer Mark Wohlers, which indirectly led to my connecting with Steve Blass.

FOREWORD by STEVE BLASS

Richard Crowley came to Florida looking for Mark Wohlers during spring training in 1998. Instead, he found me. He helped me find my way to enjoy being back in the middle of a baseball diamond again. It finally came to pass on January 30, 2005 at the Pirates' Fantasy camp where I pitched nine innings without a hitch. It was a return to the joy I always had pitching at any level during my career.

My journey has been well documented. A fine major league career: 10 major league seasons; over 100 wins; an All-Star selection; a second place Cy Young finish; and, a terrific World Series performance. Suddenly, all of that was followed by a loss of control causing a much too early departure from professional baseball.

During that freefall I tried everything to come back and throw strikes. Nothing worked, but I felt I had to exhaust every possibility. I didn't want to wonder later whether I had given up too soon and overlooked the one possibility that would have made a difference.

I got to the point where I rationalized that perhaps my allotted time as a major league player was 10 years. But it still gnawed at me that I never knew why -- why this had happened.

Dozens of well intentioned people offered suggestions to me after my baseball career. But what struck me when I met Richard was that he said he wasn't particularly interested in the whys and wherefores of this "thing." He just said, "Let's get rid of the damn thing."

I've never been one to over-analyze things. My style is just wing it and trust my instincts to get the job done. Maybe it was the right time or maybe enough time had passed (25 or so years), but Richard's responses struck a cord with me. My gut feeling, combined with the urge to throw batting practice, pitch in the old-timer games or even just play catch, made me receptive to him.

Working with Richard's technique brought about mind-shifting revelations that made playing baseball possible again; this is the heart of *Mentalball*.

I love being around positive people who aren't afraid to try things; Richard Crowley is one of those people. He's confident in his abilities and he's not afraid to take a shot at something he believes in. I believe in Richard, and I have all the confidence he can help many more as he has helped me. --- Steve Blass

FOREWORD by SHAWN GREEN

During the baseball season of 2003, I was trying to work through an injury to my right shoulder. It was a nagging injury that would pop up occasionally throughout my career, but it had finally gotten to a level in which it wouldn't subside.

It was the type of injury that only hindered my swing, it didn't completely prevent me from playing. So, I played the entire season with it, and my production at the plate declined considerably. I kept thinking I could work around it, but in the end I wasn't able to swing the bat in the same manner that I previously had.

When the season was over, the shoulder was surgically repaired, and I was ready to go for the 2004 season. This next year, however, I was still recovering from the injury in more ways than I had realized. I was improving physically each month, yet I was having difficulties recapturing the swing I had had prior to the injury. No matter what I tried, I couldn't find it, and once again I was struggling at the plate.

Halfway through that season, I came into contact with Richard. I was terribly frustrated at the time we first spoke because nothing was helping my downward spiral. He explained to me that my shoulder was physically healed, but we still had to remove a "splinter" from my psyche that was lingering because of the injury.

We did some work over the phone that first day, and I went out that night and had a breakout game against the Giants that started to turn my season around. We worked together over the phone for the rest of that year and my production for the second half was right on par with my best seasons.

I've always been a person who has searched for new ideas and has welcomed "alternative" methods in baseball and in life. Yet, at the same time, I'm very skeptical as I explore these different frontiers. I can honestly say that Richard's techniques have been very helpful to me, and I will continue to work through slumps and injuries with his help.

I've come to realize that there are intangible forces or energies that greatly affect performance. In baseball, you can show up to the stadium one day in the middle of a great hot streak, get in the batting cage, and all of a sudden feel completely lost. You look at yourself in the mirror and say, "Where did it go?"

Believe me, every player you watch on TV experiences these very feelings numerous times throughout their careers. Every golfer on the planet has gone to hit balls, only to feel as if they've never swung a club before.

The opposite is also true. An athlete can go from being "lost" to being "locked in" from one day to the next. Baseball is a constant struggle, as is life, but I feel as though Richard has discovered a way to grab hold of an intangible "opponent" that plagues all of us.

By working through our own individual challenges, we can free ourselves of some burdens and allow our natural abilities to take over. Just like a car, we constantly need our tune-ups if we want to run smoothly.

Believe me, competing is much more enjoyable and rewarding when we feel focused, relaxed, and free. --- Shawn Green

WHO CAN BENEFIT
FROM THIS BOOK

"Vision is the art of seeing things invisible." --- Jonathan Swift

Baseball players at every level struggle with their unexplainable mechanics from time to time.

How can they be hot one day and cold the next?

How can they perform so well in practice and so poorly in games?

How do they go from mound presence to mound pressure in the blink of an eye?

How do they suddenly "forget" their mechanics?

Mentalball offers the missing piece to these puzzles. It is an effective solution to what baseball has come to believe as virtually unsolvable.

- Mentalball is for little leaguers through major leaguers whose inconsistent mechanics continue despite numerous attempts to resolve them.

- Mentalball is for parents who don't want their children to lose their hopes and dreams because their problems appear unsolvable. Now, there is a solution.

- Mentalball is for teams whose goals are to have their players confident and functioning at peak performance. Now, that opportunity is available.

- Mentalball is for coaches who have exhausted their funds of knowledge, yet, are unable to help their struggling players. Now, there is a remedy.

- Mentalball is for scouts who have identified outstanding prospects only to have them collapse under pressure. Now, they no longer have to pass on them.

- Mentalball is for major and minor league organizations who want to retain struggling top prospects and veteran players when they are at a loss of what to do next. Now, that choice is possible.

Mentalball intentionally presents an abundance of players' personal stories to underscore the pervasiveness of perplexing mechanics that exists among all players from time to time. It demonstrates that any frustrating problems players encounter can successfully be conquered, thus giving players at every level hope that they too can prevail.

Mentalball is a tailor-made process for each individual player. It is not a "How To" book. It does not present a series of specific steps as solutions to problematic mechanics. That would be like reading a book on brain surgery, then suggesting readers operate on themselves. It is, and always will be, a one-on-one intervention provided by persons well-versed in its methodology.

INTRODUCTION

IT'S YOUR DREAM

"There are some people who live in a dream world, and there are some who face reality, and then there are those who turn one into the other." --- Douglas Everett

Never say never. Never give up your dream. NEVER! There definitely is a solution to any of your mechanics that don't make sense. The problem is not you, even though you may be convinced it is. The problem and solution reside in a place you are about to discover. It is the last place you would ever have expected to unravel your mechanical woes so you can play consistently, confidently and have fun again.

Think of you and your frustrating mechanics as a turtle that has been flipped on its back. None of the turtle's abilities can be actualized in such a perplexing position.

However, all that needs to be done is to get the turtle right-side-up again. Once it is accomplished, the turtle knows everything it needs to do to get on with its life. You don't have to re-teach or remind the turtle what came naturally before it got flipped over.

The same is true for you. The mental mechanics approach of Mentalball can help you get right-side-up too. And in doing so, you are automatically reconnected to everything you knew before your mechanical problems began.

Mentalball clearly demonstrates that "something else" is orchestrating your mental barriers, mystifying struggles and inconsistent mechanics that occur suddenly and for no logical reason.

Mentalball points the accusatory finger squarely at the true culprit, your "invisible opponent." Your invisible opponent is like a "psychic virus" that infects the human mind's software, much like a computer virus does.

Your physical mechanics are the visible. Your mental mechanics are the invisible. Making the invisible visible, reconnecting to your natural mechanics -- and having fun again -- is the intention of Mentalball.

CHAPTER ONE

THE INEXPLICABLE

"You never want to talk about it because back deep in your mind you're afraid it could happen to you." --- Greg Maddux

What is the cause of the Steve Blass disease? The Steve Sax syndrome? Chuck Knoblauch's epic unraveling? Rick Ankiel's meltdown? Mackey Sasser's double-pumping? Kevin Saucier's fear of hitting a batter? Mark Wohlers' inability to find the strike zone ?

What is the cause of the Monster? The Thing? The Yips? The Psychic Virus? The Creature? The Disconnect? The Little Man on your shoulder?

Baseball considers the cause as inexplicable, and rightfully so. It is mysterious, bizarre, puzzling, perplexing, weird, enigmatic, confusing, embarrassing, and frustrating.

Once injuries and medical problems have been ruled out as the source of a player's unexplainable mechanics, coaching is the primary solution. If problems persist, then players or teams may consult a sports psychologist. However, if the confusing mechanics continue, it remains a mystifying problem for the player as well as the coaches and organizations.

A player may find himself lost in the no-man's-land of the inexplicable. The more you try to figure it out, the worse it seems to

get. The more you try to understand it, the more entrenched you become in your problem.

WHEN YOU AGONIZE YOU ANALYZE

The last thing you want is your mind overloaded with analysis and clutter. Ryan Johannes, a sophomore and first baseman from Pierce College in Washington, contacted me with this very problem:

"I have been playing baseball ever since I can remember. It's always been my best sport. Just over the past year or so I've starting experiencing throwing problems.

My parents and I traced this back to an event that occurred my senior season in high school when I made a bad throw back to the pitcher and a runner on third scored on the play while our third baseman was injured trying to slide and back up the throw.

Ever since that play I always lobbed the ball back to the pitcher and have never tried to throw it. The problem throwing persisted and started happening on all throws. I would take infield and not make one accurate throw.

I became very nervous to take infield before a game because the fans and other players would wonder what was going wrong with me. Because of this I didn't play much first base my freshman year at college and considered quitting baseball.

It got in the way of other parts of my game – it was something I was always worrying about.

I want to get rid of this problem completely so I can start having fun and enjoying baseball like I always have." --- Ryan Johannes

All the best reasoning, questioning and "whys" of a player's bizarre problems make absolutely no sense. In Ryan's case, even knowing exactly when his problem began didn't help.

It is baffling. The problem can last a short period of time or it may continue for weeks, months or even years. The worst cases have even closed the door on players' careers.

The inexplicable appears to come out of the blue for no rhyme or reason. And like a torrential storm that overflows river banks, it eventually recedes, but not before it takes its toll: players who can't throw the ball from second to first; outfielders who make uncharacteristic error upon error; catchers who can't throw back to the pitcher or a particular baseman; hitters who can't lock in at the plate; and pitchers who can't focus and become consistently inconsistent.

It makes players literally forget how to throw and hit the ball. It's crazy-making. It sucks the confidence and fun out of a player and sometimes drops him into a deep, dark hole of despair -- questioning himself over and over.

It isn't limited to elite players like former New York Yankees second baseman Chuck Knoblauch either. The case of this mystifying phenomenon displaced a young college student, Rich McGinnis, from playing his favorite positions also.

THE BALL FEELS LIKE A FOREIGN OBJECT

"I read the article about you in the Pittsburgh Post-Gazette regarding "Steve Blass Disease." I'm a 22-year-old college student who has been battling the "monster" for the past five or six years.

I first started having trouble my junior year of high school. I'd given up basketball so I could concentrate full time on baseball. I worked extremely hard all winter and had high expectations for the spring. I was a pitcher and a third baseman. I would struggle all year over simple throws from third base.

I also had a rough year pitching. I had shoulder problems unrelated to the monster that rendered me ineffective. I eventually lost my starting job at third and on the mound.

In the summer I started working out behind the plate. I'd caught when I was younger. I enjoyed a very good summer catching without any hints of the monster. However, early spring the monster would rear its ugly head again. I started having trouble throwing the ball back to the pitcher. I had no problems throwing to the bases or making quick snap throws, only when I had a lot of time.

I resembled Mackey Sasser when he would attempt throwing the ball back to the pitcher. I tried every conceivable mannerism to aid in my throw. I would pump two or three times; flop around behind the plate; crawl back and forth; and finally would walk out a few feet in front of the plate before lobbing the ball back.

After high school I tried out at college as a pitcher but didn't make it. My shoulder was still messed up and I opted to see an orthopedic. Two shoulder surgeries later I attempted to come back and pitch, but my arm wasn't where it should be.

I began coaching my hometown's American Legion team. I really enjoyed coaching. I hadn't seen the monster in two years, until this summer. I was throwing batting practice when all of a sudden I started having trouble. As we got deeper into the summer, I got worse.

The monster was back.

I leaned on the sore arm crutch to avoid a compete meltdown. I never had trouble throwing strikes before. I was losing some of my passion for the game. People who have never experienced this don't understand. It's not as simple as 'Don't think. Just throw.'

It's embarrassing. And it isn't nerves. I've been in some pressure-packed situations in baseball and have come through without a problem.

That's what makes this so frustrating and difficult. It's so simple and requires virtually no high degree of skill. When I'd go to throw, I'd feel totally unconnected with the ball. I couldn't feel the ball (if that makes sense).

Before I had the problem, I could feel the ball right off the finger tips....it was like an extension of my arm. When I have trouble, it's like a foreign object.

I was commonly told, 'You're your worst enemy.'" --- Rich McGinnis

Little leaguers through pro ball players find their mechanics freezing up. Nothing flows. Arms feel robotic. Tense. Tight. Unfamiliar.

The inexplicable had been called a beast. It's been called a monster. It's been diagnosed as a "disease" without a cure. It bullies some players out of their favorite positions: it sends second baseman to the outfield; catchers to third base; and starting aces to the bullpen.

NO PRODUCTIVE ADVICE HOW TO FIX IT

Blake Miller, a college pitcher, was struggling with the mental aspects of his game. Previous help provided information, but no solutions:

"I am a sophomore at Coker College. I've had trouble with my pitching for the last few years and have actively been looking for help for my mental problem. I have always been told that I do not pitch up to my potential and that it is due to a mental problem.

The problem is that as helpful as my coaches are at pointing out problems, they have yet to give me any productive advice for how to fix it.

I usually pitch well in the bullpen, but then I am unable to transfer it to the mound. I have read books and consulted coaches, but have been unable to translate it into anything productive." --- Blake Miller

Ryan Johannes, Rich McGinnis and Blake Miller resolved their problems with the intervention of the Mentalball approach. Their complete stories can be found in Appendix B.

During the summer of 2000, New York Yankees manager Joe Torre commented on David Cone's baffling struggles on the mound that eventually contributed to ending Cone's career: *"Right now his struggles are with himself. He didn't have very good command. It seems like he's trying too hard. I'm sure a lot of things are going through his mind right now."*

Torre came to the conclusion: *"There is no cure-all answer for this."*

Sports writer Paul White agreed with this belief held by most, if not all, of baseball: *"There's no known cure for the control of yips beyond experience."*

Former New York Mets general manager Frank Cashen remarked on the unexplainable loss a player's control: *"I've seen it before. I really don't have any answers. Probably the most unfortunate thing about it is that the people who have it very seldom are cured."*

And so the "no cure" myth is perpetuated, believed and feared by athletes, coaches and management alike.

CHAPTER TWO

POSTER BOY FOR THE INEXPLICABLE

"Thought and analysis are powerless to pierce the great mystery that hovers over the world and over our existence." --- Dr. Albert Schweitzer

Former Pirates' pitcher Steve Blass, one of baseball's best clutch pitchers, helped bring a World Series championship to Pittsburgh. *"He was one of the top five pitchers in the game,"* says former Colorado Rockies' hitting coach Milt May, who was the Pirates' catcher at the time.

During the 1971 World Series, the heavily favored Baltimore Orioles jumped to a 2-0 series lead. They had a pitching trio of Jim Palmer, Dave McNally, and Mike Cuellar who were considered the best 1-2-3 punch in baseball. In addition, they had future Hall of Famers Brooks and Frank Robinson. While the underdog Pirates had all time greats Roberto Clemente and Willie Stargell, their pitching could simply not measure up to the powerful Orioles.

Enter Steve Blass, Game 3.

Blass shut down the powerful Baltimore lineup, giving up just three hits in a 5-1 home win. The victory drove the Pirates to three straight wins before Baltimore won Game six and forced a deciding Game seven.

Enter Steve Blass, Game 7.

Blass silenced the Baltimore bats, as well as their fervent fans, giving up just four hits in a complete game, 3-1 victory. The Pirates became the World Series Champions and Steve Blass stood on top of the baseball world.

However, by 1973 Blass' career imploded. He inexplicably lost control of his arm at the age of 31. Without warning, he couldn't throw a ball over the plate. It was a mystery to him, Pittsburgh, and baseball. It remained a mystery for 24 years.

Blass pitched well in warm-ups, but threw wildly the moment a game began. Blass never had a sore arm when struggling in 1973, '74 and '75. His arm was examined several times and nothing was found physically or medically wrong. In 1973 Blass went just 3-9 with a 9.85 ERA, issuing 84 walks in 88 innings.

During spring training in 1974 Blass said: *"You have no idea how frustrating it is. You don't know where you're going to throw the ball. You're afraid you might hurt someone. You know you're embarrassing yourself, but you can't do anything about it. You're helpless. Totally afraid and helpless."*

Blass continued struggling through '74 and by spring training '75 he knew his career was over. He threw his last pitch from the mound at McKechnie Field in Bradenton, Florida. *"When it was gone, it was gone for good,"* Blass said. *"To this day, I don't know what caused it."*

Former Pirates' catcher, Manny Sanguillen, praised his friend: *"Steve Blass was able to do anything. When he was pitching, the ball would move everywhere. He was smart, too. He would be able to see what the hitters did and be able to locate the ball at the right place at the proper time.*

And then it was all gone, just like that."

Blass tried more than two hundred suggestions and approaches including hypnosis and transcendental meditation to resolve his bizarre loss of the strike zone. All attempts were in vain.

Blass' problem was considered incurable. His mysterious struggles were dubbed the "Steve Blass disease." Subsequent pitchers whose mechanics fell through that same hole into the Alice in Wonderland world of bizarreness and confusion were consequently labeled as having the Steve Blass disease. Most notable were Mark Wohlers when he was with the Atlanta Braves and Cincinnati Reds, and Rick Ankiel of the St. Louis Cardinals.

And so the seeds were sown in baseball's mentality and took root. It sprouted into new beliefs and a new vocabulary of "disease", "inexplicable" and "incurable." And up until now, it has had quite a following.

Twenty-four years later I met Steve Blass quite by accident during spring training of '98. I had traveled to Florida expressly to connect with Atlanta Braves closer Mark Wohlers and offer my services. However, it was destined for me to meet and work with Blass rather than Wohlers at that time. A year later, Steve felt confident enough to go public with the work we did. It appeared in Paul Myers' article in the *Pittsburgh Post-Gazette* April 25, 1999 entitled:

WILL BLASS FINALLY GET A GRIP ON BASEBALL?

A psychologist from Taos, N.M., who was trying to find and help Mark Wohlers in spring training might instead be helping Steve Blass exorcise the demons that painfully and prematurely ended the Pirates' broadcaster's pitching career in 1975. Richard Crowley is the man's name.

But Blass had never heard of him until one morning midway through spring training in Bradenton. "He'd been trying to see Wohlers and kept missing him," Blass said. "He told me everything he'd read about Wohlers had my

11

name in it. He said it almost seemed that he was more meant to see me."
Maybe. For sure, Blass' problem has had a longer life.

While Wohlers still has a chance to correct his control problems and pitch effectively again in the major leagues, Blass never had a chance. He walked away from the game in spring training, 1975--when he still should have been in the prime of his career--and never really threw a baseball again in any meaningful way.

Until now.

That morning in Bradenton, Blass and Crowley talked for perhaps 90 minutes. "He asked me if I wanted to explore getting rid of the problem," Blass said. "I'd been approached by hundreds of people over the years, and so I asked him a lot of questions. He came up with pretty good responses. I was impressed with him.

I don't want to get into a lot of what he said. That's his thing. But he called it a 'psychic virus.' He said, 'The thing to do is to get rid of it and replace it with something positive.'"

Blass took two days to think all this through. He had to battle against hope that maybe, perhaps, finally, he could pick up a baseball again and throw it where he wanted to, without worrying about hitting a batter.

He met Crowley again. "We talked for maybe an hour and a half, and then he left and went back to Taos," Blass said. A day or so later, Blass picked up a ball and a glove and played catch with fellow broadcaster Bob Walk behind the Pirates' clubhouse at McKechnie Field.

He threw fastballs.
He threw sliders.
. He smiled.

"It felt pretty good," Blass said. "I'd forgotten how much I missed just throwing a baseball."

A few days later, Blass arranged to meet with Nashville Manager Trent Jewett at the minor-league complex at 7 a.m. Jewett, a former catcher, agreed to catch Blass, who threw from a mound for the first time in 24 years. That, too, went well.

"I didn't feel the anxiety and the tenseness when I was ready to release the ball," Blass said.

But the big test was yet to come. How would Blass react when a "batter" stood at the plate? He would learn several days later.

Crowley flew back to Bradenton. The two met at the minor-league complex, and Blass threw from the edge of a mound in a batting cage--with Crowley standing in the batter's box.

"I did hit him once," Blass said. "But it was all right to keep going. I threw 80 balls, and I'd say 80 percent of them were where I wanted to throw them."

"I had missed it more than I thought," he said. "I don't feel anxiety, but this is just the beginning of the process. I have no illusions about this.

I just want to be able to throw a baseball. If it worked into something where I could throw batting practice, that would be good, but...Just throwing again is something. I don't know if it's a big deal, but it's a nice thing. And I'm amazed at how good my arm feels. Well, after all... my arm should feel good after 24 years' rest."

A LETTER FROM BLASS

Thirty years after Steve Blass left the mound, he returned to it once again, and victoriously. Reflecting upon this event, Steve sent me the following personal letter:

"In my particular case in the past, I would tense up as I prepared to release the ball in a wind up. The elimination of that tension and seizing up was the

whole key. I still have apprehension when I walk out to the mound, but now I can release the ball free and easy.

Hell, I never did have arm problems during my career. So when I pitched nine innings January 30 at the 2005 Pirates Fantasy camp, the first time in 30 years, it was a return to the joy I always had pitching at any level during my career.

I can't possibly overstate what that Fantasy Camp outing meant to me. The day's format is for each of the eight 'camper' teams to play a three-inning game against the major leagues. I had not planned to pitch, but one camper challenged me to pitch just to him. When he came up to bat I threw just two or three warm up pitches because I thought I'd just go out there, get it done quickly and come out.

With that being said, I was still quite nervous, but when the first pitch went alright, I said 'Let's turn it loose again.' That pitch was fine too. I finished the game by pitching 8 2/3 innings. As each inning went by my confidence increased and a great feeling came over me. I was having the time of my life out there and one of the greatest things about the whole situation was that my old Pirates teammates were enjoying it almost as much as I was.

Even though it was 'just' a Fantasy Camp experience, I will never forget that day. I feel like it has given me a degree of closure and triumph after all these many years, and I feel you helped me get to that point." --- Steve Blass

CHAPTER THREE

YOUR INVISIBLE OPPONENT

The "Little Man" on Your Shoulder
The Steve Blass Disease
The Psychic Virus
The Disconnect
The Creature
The Monster
The Demon
The Thing
The Yips
"It"

"The purpose of poetry is to remind us that there are no doors and windows, and that uninvited guests come in and out at will." --- Milosz Czeslaw

Your invisible opponent is illustrated in the allegory of a toad preparing to cross a wide river. As he was ready to jump into the water he became tense upon hearing a chilling voice. He turned around and realized the voice belonged to a scorpion.

The scorpion said, "I need your help."

The toad replied, "I don't trust you at all," and moved further away.

The scorpion begged the toad to take him across the river as he couldn't swim and desperately needed to get to the other side.

The toad said, "All you want to do is kill me. I'm no fool."

The scorpion pointed out the logic of why he would not kill the toad as he had no other way to cross the river. Finally, the toad was convinced. Before long the toad was carrying the scorpion on his back swimming through the waters.

Halfway across the river the toad felt a burning sensation of the scorpion's poison stinging him and he cried out, "But you told me you wouldn't harm me! Why did you do it? You will die too."

The scorpion replied simply, "Because it's my nature."

And so too it is the nature of your invisible opponent to trick you, to use logic on you and to keep your awareness diminished. It will continue to manifest itself until all *its* energy is gone.

Sometimes your invisible opponent can drag a slump on and on. Or, its energy can dissipate as suddenly as it began. Rather than waiting helplessly for its reign to end, Mentalball can put you in control -- fast.

"Something else" is at work undermining your ability to play the way you have your entire life. The responsible party is not you, but rather a separate entity altogether.

I call this "something else" your invisible opponent. It orchestrates your inconsistent mechanics from behind the scenes. It frustrates your resolve to do your best.

Your invisible opponent is likened to a psychic virus that infects your mind's software. It does it the same way that a virus can attach itself to your computer's software leaving you bewildered and frustrated. However, your imagination contains the back-up of all your mechanics' original programs.

Your invisible opponent can unravel self-affirmations and self-talk like a cat with a ball of yarn. It can convert your positive thinking into runaway negative thoughts of criticisms and self-judgments.

I CONNECTED WITH THE BALL AGAIN

Barrett Wright, a right-handed pitcher with the Tampa Bay minor leagues, struggled mightily with his wild pitching. Despite intensive coaching and positive support, Barrett often found himself living in a perplexing and agonizing world of his own:

"I can't thank Tom Foley (former Director of Minor League Operations of the Devil Rays) enough for introducing me to Dr. Crowley who did his magic that got me back pitching again.

Prior to working with Dr. Crowley I was totally out of control. Sometimes when I'd throw the ball it would end up four feet in front of me. Other times it would be all over the place. I would miss throwing to first by as much as 20 feet. I couldn't figure out what had happened with my arm. I was in a terrible place.

I couldn't believe how quickly my arm returned to normal after working with Dr. Crowley during only four days.

Halfway through his interactive techniques I knew something important had happened. Before our fourth meeting the tingling sensation in my hand had ended. I felt connected with the ball again. I stopped throwing wild.

Next my velocity returned. And finally, my confidence was back and I was able to concentrate and focus again.

After my throwing problem ended, it was as though I had never had it in the first place. I can't explain it any more than that. It just left me.

Later I would apply his techniques on my own and they worked effectively. I hope it never happens to anybody. But if it does they can get over it in a matter of days and not have to go through the humiliation and anxiety I did before I hooked up with Dr. Crowley." --- Barrett Wright

Your invisible opponent can do to you what kryptonite does to Superman. When you find yourself in actual games, it absorbs your energy leaving you depleted of resources and exhausted of alternatives. You are beside yourself.

Until now there has been no one to blame except yourself. But that has all changed with Mentalball. You don't have to be the fall-guy any longer once you recognize it is the invisible opponent setting you up to take the fall.

Your invisible opponent lulls you and seduces you into thinking *its* thoughts are your thoughts; *its* beliefs are your beliefs. It talks you into certain behaviors and out of others, contrary to what is best for you. It is its job. It is its intent. It is its nature. It is a good con artist.

Your invisible opponent works like an internal ventriloquist. It makes *you* appear to be the one thinking *its* negative thoughts -- ones that tense your body and interfere with your concentration during a game.

It convinces you to accept what you are thinking as your own thoughts and beliefs. When in truth, they are being "mouthed" from behind the scenes by your invisible opponent – making you blame yourself. It has you falsely thinking and saying: "I'm creating my throwing problems. I'm responsible for all my technical difficulties. I'm sabotaging my game."

Your invisible opponent can even make you forget your mechanics. It makes you feel bad when it reminds you what you could have done or should have done differently during a game. It beats you up with its weapon of hindsight. It is very convincing now, isn't it? It's very good at what it does.

Until you dismantle it.

The invisible opponent, as ventriloquist, is not the voice of your intuition. Intuition speaks to you in a quiet voice -- a whisper at times. Intuition never judges you. It supports and guides you. It nudges you with a word or a phrase or a sentence at the most. Intuition doesn't repeat itself or harp on things as your invisible opponent does.

Any voice that is not positive and supportive of you -- even in the worst of times -- is not your intuition.

THE ANXIETY IS GONE

Kevin McKernan's invisible opponent had him believing that he was the one responsible for putting pressure on himself and initiating his negative thoughts:

"I am a 29-year-old catcher for a semi-pro team in PA (Bulldogs). I was a three-time, 1st team all-league and a two-time all-city. I got a contract offer by the Chicago Cubs out of high school, played four years in college, and was brought up to Yankee Stadium to work out for the GM when I froze up.

I went to see a sports psychologist this winter and we talked a couple of times. I also have been reading books about the mental side of the game.

As for throwing, that has been tough. I have had bits and pieces of this problem for a long time dating back to high school. I have always put that extra pressure on myself to perform at a high level.

But this year and last year have been the worst. I freeze whenever I have to make a play. I think the negative of "Can I make it?"

Kevin had done everything players and organizations believe can be done to resolve such puzzling conflicts. He saw a sports psychologist, read books on the subject, received good coaching and practiced visualizations. But he couldn't remove the psychic virus that invaded his confidence and mechanics because his invisible opponent still had a grip on his arm.

We worked three times over the phone on things such as his release point difficulties, pressure and nervousness, thinking negatively, worrying about disappointing others, his specific memory of freezing Yankee Stadium and more. Kevin's imagination worked for him and he emailed me these results:

"Things feel better out there. The anxiety is gone. I try to use that mental image as often as I can when I am in different situations.

I have been throwing better because I have more confidence. I've been hosing the ball…even in the bullpen. Guys on the team are amazed at how I am gunning the ball around the infield for warm ups. Thanks so much." --- Kevin McKernan

CHAPTER FOUR

UNMASKING YOUR INVISIBLE OPPONENT

"Even if one is unconscious of *something*, however, that *something* still lives in the person and through him in the world." --- Mary Watkins

Carl Jung, the eminent Swiss psychologist, envisioned the process of *growing into consciousness* as a progression towards becoming responsible for one's self, for what comes to be through one's living.

Believing you control all your thoughts and are completely responsible for them is a myth.

It goes hand in hand with the false notion that you, and you alone, intentionally create all your problems, illnesses, bad relationship, choices, etc. These guilt-producing beliefs have been embraced by mainstream society as strongly as previous societies held fast to the belief that the world was flat. The invisible opponent has been very convincing over the centuries.

How do you begin to unmask your invisible opponent and remove yourself as the responsible party for your mechanical issues? Begin by increasing your consciousness.

Start by paying *attention* to conversations with yourself and others. In that way you can change the grammatical structure.

Examples of changing grammatical structure in your thoughts and conversations would be the following: Instead of expressing, "I'm becoming my own worst enemy," change it to the truth: "Something else, and not me, makes me believe I'm becoming my own worst enemy."

Instead of thinking, "I doubt myself on every pitch," change it to the truth: "Something else, and not me, makes me doubt myself on every pitch."

Instead of believing, "No matter what I do I'm never good enough," change it to the truth: "Something else, and not me, makes me believe no matter what I do I am never good enough."

Or change other false beliefs of blaming yourself from "I'm at fault when I lose; there's nobody else to blame than myself," to the truth: "Something else, and not me, falsely blames me when my mechanics aren't doing what I intend them to do."

If it is your conscious intention to play badly, then you are at fault. You are completely responsible. However, I've never met a player whose intention was to fail. Remember, the key word here is INTENTION.

Is it your intention to have those thoughts that are beating you up? No. Do you want them? No. Then don't buy the belief that you, and you alone, are pulling them in; that you are guilty for their being there; nor that you can effortlessly remove them and replace them with positive thoughts.

Can you get rid of them with positive thoughts? Maybe. But not as easily if it is a prank of your imagination, and the prankster is your invisible opponent.

That's why those thoughts can come right back into your head because something else is at work. See how long it is before those unwanted thoughts pop back in again like a melody you can't shake loose. Maybe you fall asleep with those thoughts. Or you get up in the middle of the night and there they are. Or they are still playing an encore the moment you wake up.

So you may well ask, "If I am not *intending* to struggle at the plate or when throwing the ball, then who is? There's nobody else in here besides me. Right?"

Wrong!

Something else from another place in your consciousness is orchestrating your malady. Your invisible opponent makes you battle and blame yourself as being completely responsible for your slumps and struggles -- the last thing from the truth.

Ask any player if he is aware when he is struggling that something else, something weird is going on in a way he can't quite put into words. You will notice his head nodding even if he can't find the words to express it.

Historically, baseball has viewed your mechanics as the primary cause. However, somewhere in the back of your head, the only one who knows your problem is not simply mechanics, *per se*, is you.

Yet you have a difficult time getting others to experience what it is like to walk in your shoes. If they did, they would drop the observable mechanics as being the real issue and understand that something else is underlying your mechanical inconsistencies.

Former New York Yankees second baseman Chuck Knoblauch expressed his frustration when he was battling his invisible opponent: "If it was as simple as going out and doing it, it would have happened."

Former Los Angeles Dodgers first baseman/outfielder Shawn Green was astute when he said, *"Everyone from the outside seems to have all the* answers when you're struggling. Everyone tries to break it down into being some small mechanical flaw or something like that, **but there's always more to it."**

ABLE TO BOUNCE BACK

Hector Nelo, a high school pitcher from Miami, was aware of when his problem began, but he couldn't locate his mechanics as pressure had separated him from them. He wrote me the following:

"My biggest problem that I see affecting my performance is not being able to bounce back after an error, or after a walk, or just some kind of failure in the game. It's also the pressure of wanting to do good, and the pressure of the people who want me to do good.

What might have caused the problem was that at the end of my sophomore year was when we were eliminated in the regional semi-finals. I came in to relieve. There was one out. Man on first. And there were a lot of people (I'm not going to lie to you, I was pretty nervous) and we were winning 5-to-3. So, I walked the first batter. Then I walked the second, and I was taken out.

I had just come from throwing a no-hitter in Tennessee on a tournament during spring break that year and it was my second time that I was going to pitch in varsity. Then we lost. And that kind of stuck with me.... that chance that we could have won the game."

We worked a couple of times two weeks apart on a number of problems Hector introduced: unable to bounce back after a mistake; angry and disappointed with himself when he walked a hitter; pressure to do good; and lack of confidence following removal from a varsity game.

As we were finishing the first session during which we engaged his imagination, Hector excitedly said that he wanted to play right away. He said, *"I feel like a 'Super Hero' and that I can do anything now."* He sent the following updates of his progression:

Emailed February 28:

"Well, it went great. It was a big improvement. I threw two walks, but I was able to bounce back and make quality pitches to get out the innings. I threw three innings with no hits. And once again I was able to keep my focus and keep doing good. So I'm very happy with the results. (By the way the walks weren't consecutives; they were with good pitches that the batter was able to lay off)."

Emailed April 11:

"My season has been great. Our team had four no-hitters in the year and two of them are mine. I don't mean to brag, but I'm doing really good compared to the years before. I was named for the All-Tournament team because of that.

I appreciate the help that you gave me in just two hours over the phone with the steps you walked me through. It made a huge difference in my performance. I've been blowing guys away and it feels good. My game came back. I can't thank you enough." --- Hector Nelo

When you become more conscious, you begin to see more of what has been in front of you all along. Of all places, it is actually your imagination that can increase your conscious awareness and have you playing in the moment, the here and now.

Research by Drs. Michael Greenwood and Peter Nunn in *Paradox and Healing* points to a similar conclusion: *"We find that healing occurs while we are in altered states of consciousness, a state in which we are focused in the present moment. Past and future are somehow dissolved and exist with us in the present. Explanations are not only difficult but somehow redundant. The experience of healing speaks for itself."*

CHAPTER FIVE

THE CROWLEY METHOD
AND MENTALBALL

"The prime factor preventing the [healing] experience was intellect control, so we posited that if we could find a technique to shift the focus of the intellect temporarily, more people might break into a significant experience."
--- Michael Greenwood and Peter Nunn

A long, long time ago, a horse and rider came upon a man on his hands and knees desperately combing the ground.

When the rider inquired as to the problem, the man said, "I have lost a very important key. This key is to a chest which contains documents I need tomorrow. Without them I will suffer grave consequences."

The man dismounted and joined in the search. Later, a second horseman came by and also helped in the hunt for the key.

Eventually a third rider approached, and hearing the man's plight, offered his assistance as well. "However," he said to the desperate man in need of this all important key, "I have one question. Exactly where were you when you lost the key?"

The man pointed to a location some distance away from where they were all franticly searching. It was an unknown territory at the forest's edge, thick with trees. The third rider asked, "Why, pray tell, are you looking here and not there for your key?"

The man replied, "Well....first of all the light is better here."

Most people are unaccustomed to looking for solutions in the illogical, irrational area of their mind -- their imagination. Yet, it is the imagination where problems can originate. Only because the light appears better in the familiar territory of logic do we refrained from enlisting the right side of the brain to resolve problems.

I created the Crowley Method from my own intuition and inventive imagination while engaged in a year long tutorial with Clara Stuart Flagg on the subject of lucid dreaming.

Lucid dreams refer to dream-states in which you are aware you are having a dream *at that very moment in time* you are in it. By lucid dreaming, you learn to control the outcome. Fear-ridden dreams don't run you. You run the dreams. Conquering the fears and anxieties contained in your dreams translates favorably into your external life.

I never came close to having a lucid dream. I did, however, learn many things Clara had to teach. She passed on a fund of knowledge developed by her deceased husband, Kilton Stuart, a psychologist from Great Britain. He had traveled around the world nine times asking indigenous peoples to share their dreams and fantasies.

Stuart encountered one remote tribe in the Philippines called the Senoi (pronounced Sen-noy.) The Senoi were illiterate pigmies, possibly the most primitive group on earth. However, they possessed knowledge which the rest of the civilized world had not discovered. They were known as "the dream tribe." After studying their ways, Stuart believed he had found Utopia.

For over 300 hundred years, the Senoi tribe had no murders, no warfare with other tribes, no jails, and no mental health problems. Their secret? Every morning the elders would meet with the children and have them relate their dreams from the night before.

The elders taught the children how to become conscious and "awake" while dreaming. They were taught how to resolve their everyday problems and emotional reactions by "laundering" them every night in their dream-world. In this way, every day was a new day and they would not have to act out negatively on themselves, family members or other tribes.

The children were taught to engage dream-characters and invite them to become allies. For example, if being chased by a tiger, they were instructed to approach the tiger and offer it a gift. If the tiger was benevolent and accepted the gift, they then had the tiger's energy as a dream-helper and an ally. They would then ask the tiger to give them a song, dance, or a solution to a problem which they would share with the tribe the next morning.

However, if the tiger refused to become an inner ally and continued threatening them, the children were taught to conquer the opposing energy of the tiger and make its energy work on their behalf. They were instructed to annihilate any hostile dream-characters and replace them with positive ones.

The Senoi experience became the illusive missing piece to the therapeutic puzzle for healing and remedying our human condition. It was the missing link that changed how I would work with clients in the future.

After Clara's lucid dream course, I was so indoctrinated in its principles that I would began to hear a friend's upset, my brother's latest golf angst or a client's problem in an entirely new way. *I heard their stories as if they were telling me a dream.*

I then began to have them view their problem as being a "dream-character." I enlisted their imagination in the form of "conscious dreaming" to meet and resolve their problems. Thus, the Crowley Method evolved.

MENTALBALL

Mentalball is about the spine of sports. It supports the rest of the body of your mechanics. Using its knowledge can help you overcome all odds, conquer your personal demons and return you to being relaxed, focused, and consistent.

Mentalball is the specific application of the Crowley Method to baseball as well as other sports. Mentalball is a tailor-made procedure for athletes wanting to enhance their performance. And equally, if not more importantly, Mentalball is a ground-breaking approach that is an effective remedy for perplexing challenges faced by every athlete, whether mechanical or mental in nature.

Before I work with players, I have them email me as much detail as possible how they are experiencing their struggles, when it began, and what steps they have taken to correct it. At the same time they are instructed to go to my website www.sportsmaker.com and complete the online self-assessment survey entitled 100 Challenges Players Can Conquer, found in Appendix A. It will give you an idea of the types of problems that Mentalball's approach can help triumph over -- even if you have been convinced otherwise.

Procedurally, I take an athlete's baffling problems and make them visible by entering his imagination. I have the player suspend logic for a moment and ask his imagination for spontaneous images producing the various problems that have disconnected him from his mechanics and confidence.

The imagination always complies with the requested images. It is its intention to help. I then have the player communicate internally, telepathically, with the images using specifically designed questions.

The image has a consciousness of its own and responds to a player's communication with it. It is the response of the image, and not what the player thinks it means, that tells me the next question for the player to ask the image. I am like a director of a movie in a player's imagination.

During this process, a "shift" within the imagination occurs which "re-wires" and "re-awakens" the player to his or her original natural mechanics -- effortlessly and spontaneously.

CHAPTER SIX

IMAGINATION

"Imagination is more important than knowledge. It is the preview of life's coming attractions." --- Albert Einstein

One evening an old Cherokee told his grandson about a battle that goes on inside people.

He said, "My son, the battle is between two wolves. One is Evil. It is anger, envy, sorrow, regret, greed, arrogance, self-pity, guilt, resentment, inferiority, lies, false pride, superiority and ego.

The other is Good. It is joy, peace, love, hope, serenity, humility, kindness, benevolence, empathy, generosity, truth, compassion and faith."

The grandson thought about if for a minute and the asked his grandfather, "Which wolf wins?"

The old Cherokee replied, "The one you feed."

Your imagination may be the last place you would ever have considered looking for solutions to your life's struggles. By changing the symbolic images in your imagination that literally and figuratively preview your life's coming attractions, you can influence "the now."

The answers to your mechanics, consistency, control and confidence lie within you. The symbolic images within your imagination reconnect you with these answers.

Your imagination is "on" every second of your life. Whether you are awake or asleep. Whether you are aware of it or not. Imagination is like an advanced intelligence that has been gifted to every human being.

Your imagination has no relationship with your I.Q., the amount of your education, nor your socio-economic status. Everyone is born with imagination. Children have it. Adults have it. Even people who are convinced they don't have any imagination, have it.

Notice how many times a day you find yourself daydreaming and fantasizing as your mind wanders from the subject at hand. This is your imagination at work.

Pay attention to how your never-ending, rambling inner conversations translate into images all the time. Simply tell somebody about some of the favorite toys you played with as a child. Or that best friend you hung out with. Or the first baseball mitt you ever got. Observe how your imagination will paint vivid images to accompany those recollections. And those listening will do likewise to process your stories.

Notice what you fantasize when your thoughts turn to baseball. Do you imagine pitching the perfect game, hitting out of the ballpark or leading your team to victory after victory?

Take a moment, and pretend being at one of your most enjoyable restaurants eating your favorite foods....

Now pretend being with your closest teammates....

Now pretend being on a date with a celebrity or star you're infatuated with....

Now pretend you're playing one of your best games where you rocked....

See how quickly the images appear without any conscious work on your part. Your imagination can also delete any unwanted images that interfere with your mechanics and replace them with positive ones. There is a formulary for doing just that. And Mentalball is it. By intentionally using your imagination, you can dramatically improve your game.

IT WAS A GOOD DAY AT THE OFFICE

Jenna Busa, a junior at UMass in Amherst, was referred by her coaches. She was a very good softball pitcher who was struggling with consistency:

"My problem is particularly with my inside fastball. It's my strongest pitch; it's the right height and has great velocity. However, during games and even during a pitching workout, I lose it. It's too low, and has no velocity at all. I could have it for one batter and punch her out, then the very next batter, not have it."

At the end of April we worked on her control problems and she contacted me with her results:

"It felt so easy for me yesterday and that's definitely something I haven't felt in a while. In general, my entire pitching workout was great. I felt so powerful and dominant towards the strike zone! I kept thinking of the exercise we did and I felt like nothing was in my way, especially with my inside fastball. All my pitches were thrown hard and accurately.

We won the first game 12-to-2. The pitcher was Barbie LaFogg, who you've worked as well. I pitched the second game. We won 9-to-0. I had a no-hitter and went 3-for-3 at the plate with two homeruns!! It was a good day at the office.

I just want to thank you from the bottom of my heart for all your help. I know we've only had one session, but just from that I feel so much better about my pitching!! There are a few things I'd like to go over regarding my curveball and change-up."

We immediately spent two additional sessions going after her curveball and change-up. By the end of May, Jenna was on a roll:

"The end of this season was absolutely spectacular!! You really helped me tap into the mental aspect of pitching that I never knew. I've gained so much confidence in myself, I feel like a whole new pitcher out there! Thanks for all you've done." --- Jenna Busa

Jenna had just one career at bat until she was inserted into the starting lineup, coincidentally, at the time we began working. She lit up at the plate like she did on the mound. Jenna's translating her frustrating mechanics into symbolic images resulted in a major shift. She was named the Louisville Slugger National Player of the Week. She was also named the Atlantic-10 Pitcher of the Week, ECAC Pitcher of the Week and UMass/Dinn Brothers Athlete of the Week.

The awards acknowledged Jenna's back-to-back no-hitters as well as batting .714 with three home runs and seven RBI. I reminded her: *"It wasn't me who did that. You did it by tapping into the resource of your imagination. I just showed you how."*

Jenna compiled a .438 batting average (7-16) on the year. She won three consecutive games in the A-10 Championship while compiling an ERA of 0.73. She was selected the A-10 Tournament Most Outstanding Player Award and was named to the A-10 Tournament All-Conference Team. After the season, she was also named a Jewish Sports Review First Team All-American.

PRANKS OF THE IMAGINATION

Carl Jung offers another way of viewing the invisible opponent's ability to preoccupy us with thoughts we wish we could eliminate. Jung sees it simply as being part of our human condition.

He recalled consulting with a professor of philosophy about his cancer phobia. The man was convinced that he had a malignant tumor even though nothing was ever found in dozens of X-rays. Even though the man agreed that he knew there is nothing there, he couldn't get the thought out of his mind that there *might* be something present.

What was it that created such a haunting idea? Jung suggested: *"It obviously came from a fear that was not instilled by conscious deliberation. The morbid thought suddenly overcame him, and it had a power of its own that he could not control."*

Jung concluded: *"It is a shattering experience for a civilized person to admit that his troubles are nothing more than a foolish prank of the imagination."*

Pranks of the imagination are illustrated in the metaphor of marionettes. Strings are controlled by a master puppeteer who remains invisible in the shadows. The only thing most of the world of sports views as *reality* is the behavior of the marionettes -- the athletes.

Whatever the "marionettes" do, the sports world accepts with applause and adoration or rejects with boos and ridicule. Their judgment is grounded in the observable, visible behavior of the marionettes, and not in the unobservable, invisible behavior of the puppeteer pulling their strings.

The world is fixated, as if in a trance, with whom it believes is the responsible party that it judges and finds guilty. Shame and blame are like spotlights wrongfully pointed at the marionettes, the athletes,

and not at the puppeteer, the invisible opponent, convincing many players to suffer in silence.

CHAPTER SEVEN

SYMBOLIC IMAGES

"Positive images of the future are a powerful and magnetic force...They draw us on and energize us, give us courage and will to take important initiatives. Negative images of the future also have magnetism. They pull the spirit downward in the path of despair." --- William James, Father of American Psychology

Jungian Marion Woodman clearly describes symbols best in the 1991 Institute of Noetic Science Review:

> *Why...is the symbol a healer? Why is the symbol in your imagination...a gift from God? The reason is this: The image works on your imagination, it works on your emotional body, it works on your thinking, and on your intellect. So for a moment your intellect, emotion, imagination are one. You are whole. The image clicks, and at that instant your whole being says, "Yes!"*

Symbolism, the universal language of the dream-world, exists in your imagination. Symbolic solutions and the opposing forces from your invisible opponent both emanate from the same source, symbolic images.

Stored in your imagination are the image-forms of all of your perceptions, beliefs, thoughts and attitudes. The solution to unexplainable mechanics exists in the multiplex cinema housed within your imagination. When you ask your imagination for an image, it will offer you one.

These image-forms are projected onto the *screen* of the every day reality of your mechanics. These image-forms literally translate into how you approach a game, your stance at the plate or your presence on the mound.

If the images contained on the *film* in your imagination's *projector* are positive and successful, you will project those pleasant experiences effortlessly onto your game. They lend to conversations you have with yourself -- encouraging and upbeat.

However, if the images are negative and fearful, your invisible opponent will project those worrisome experiences onto a specific part of your game. For example, you may be hitting very well, yet have problems throwing. The conversations you have with yourself become interspersed with doubt and second-guessing.

With Mentalball, your imagination can move symbolic images around like pieces of a puzzle. In doing so you reconnect to your mechanics without adding more suggestions or theories. The symbolic images *communicate* with your problem without adding the clutter of extra thoughts and words. You want your mind quiet and relaxed so you can focus and concentrate. And symbolic images make this possible.

It is like the adage "a picture is worth a thousand words." It gives you the wisdom of the thousand words, yet contained within one symbolic image. By dismantling your invisible opponent's problem-producing images you can then replace them with positive ones.

Once the positive image is planted into the soil of your imagination, it takes root immediately and you find your mechanics doing well again.

VASTLY IMPROVED

Christopher Light, a high school freshman, presented a perplexing problem that had paralyzed him as a catcher. He describes his problem and how the solution occurred when he transformed it into symbolic images:

"I had the chance to throw as a catcher as a freshman for my high school team. A few days before the first game while throwing in the bullpen, I couldn't throw the ball back to the pitcher. By the first game I couldn't get within 10 feet of the pitcher. I analyzed everything I could think of and still couldn't figure out what was wrong with me.

We found Dr. Crowley on the internet and my mom set up a session with him over the phone. I talked to him about an hour. I first thought his tactics seemed a little silly with his having me use symbolic images in my imagination, but I was willing to try anything.

After applying his methods, the very next day I was vastly improved. By the end of the week I was able to start as catcher and have never looked back. This past year, my junior year, my fielding percentage was .946. I now hope to play in college. Dr. Crowley gave me back my game." --- Christopher Light

CHAPTER EIGHT

VISUALIZATION

"I did my preparation in the afternoon. I liked to lay down for an hour before I went to the park. That's when I went over the pictures in my mind. We didn't call it visualizing then, but I sure used my imagination." --- Duke Snider

Many players have reported improved results when using visualization techniques. It is accomplished by repetitively picturing yourself successfully performing the acts of throwing, fielding, catching or hitting.

I recommend athletes incorporating visualization into their daily lives, if only for a few minutes while finding themselves sitting on the bench during a game or before falling asleep.

While visualization is an excellent tool, Mentalball differs dramatically from it. Mentalball is the intentional utilization of the imagination through its symbolic images to end problematic mechanics.

If you find yourself using visualization techniques without benefit, it may indicate that your invisible opponent is operating and needs to be addressed before your mental rehearsing can be effective.

When former New York Mets catcher Mackey Sasser was lost behind the plate throwing back to the pitcher he once said, *"I've been working with people on visualization. But either the throw's going to come or it's not. What can you do? Just pray."*

When former Texas Rangers catcher Mike Stanley went through a period of living in fear of simply throwing the ball, he also tried visualization. He concluded, *"All I could visualize was making an errant throw. I couldn't even visualize myself making a good one."* As for self-talk, he said, *"You can say positive things over and over again, and it won't help. You have to believe it."*

Your invisible opponent is clever enough to convince you what is not true. It is a heavy-weight champion in the art of self-doubting and second-guessing. It makes you doubt yourself when you affirm "I can lick this problem" with a converse thought or image of your striking out again or throwing the ball in the dirt.

Your imagination has the ability to transcend many issues including your lack of confidence. In a short period of time, your imagination can take those worrisome thoughts that haunt you and exchange them for feelings of inner calmness, confidence and relaxation. Imagine what it can do for your game.

I FELT AS THOUGH A BLOCKAGE WAS RELIEVED

Christopher Mitchell, a former minor league pitcher, who was struggling with his game for a number of years emailed me May 5:

"I'll give you some of the traits that I have experienced as a former minor league right-handed pitcher.

I used to throw anywhere from 89-93 mph in college (De Sales University) my sophomore and junior years. My mechanics and velocity were good and the arm was fluid. Then midway through my junior year I started trying to throw even harder to impress the 16 or so scouts' radar guns that would follow me. And over time, my mechanics mutated. I played one season in the minors and I was released after a year. I believe they thought I would hurt my arm the way I was throwing.

The following year I signed with another team in spring training and a coach tried to adjust my mechanics. I never really focused so much on mechanics until that year and I practiced each day doing their form. I started to do it correct sometimes and then I started thinking about it too much to the point where I was pausing the arm with a robotic motion. I would push off too early with my lower half while my arm drags behind.

I have since been released multiple times because I can throw well on the side. But come game situations, I would start the robotic form with mutated mechanics. Sometimes in game situations, I even drop the ball out behind my back as I break my hands to throw. It is quite embarrassing letting go of a baseball that early and I knew it wasn't because my hands were sweaty.

At times I can throw harder from center field to home than from the mound to home. When I throw correctly and in the zone my stuff is as good as the top major league pitchers. I've signed in the past with two major league affiliates and six independent teams because of my arm strength on the side mounds and different pitches, but unfortunately I'd change most everything in game settings.

I've been called the Jekyll and Hyde of pitchers. When I am focused on the batter you don't want to hit off me, but all too often over the last 4 years I've been battling myself.

My primary reason for contacting you is to get back the mental confidence and command that will help me have fun again on the mound. I need help finding the positive messages and techniques to remove past thoughts of negativity from my game. I haven't been able to find that zone or focus in years. I am struggling to visualize success prior to my actions."

Chris and I worked May 9 on the such things as: inability to feel the release point; thinking too much on the mound; analyzing himself;

worrying about what people are thinking; believing he is his worst enemy; and his body's freezing up:

Emailed May 13:
"I felt as though a blockage was relieved from the back side of my head as I was working with you. I agree with you that lots of teammates and coaches in the past would say, "Relax and don't think", but they didn't understand how to actually prevent me from thinking and locking up.

Chris had a fracture on his foot that shut him down. Even in the middle of July he was still doing physical therapy with the foot and building the muscles and tendons back up to help support the healed bone. His plans were to still play fall league. Chris remained in touch with me *via* emails such as this one on May 28:

I talked to Barclay Reynolds, former pitching coach at Swarthmore University. He doesn't understand why more teams don't tap into the mind. Another coach that worked with helping my mechanics agrees with your idea of creating an image to take the fall and creating a positive image. It may be a few weeks or a month, but I still keep fresh in my mind the images that will help me get back to me."

Christopher stayed in contact with me and we worked on and off over the next several months:

Emailed October 2:
"I have pitched in two games this fall. The first game I got a little tired by the fifth inning, but overall my control was good. The second game I threw all nine innings and struck out 12 while walking two. I thought the one walk was a strike out, but the umpire saw it otherwise.

I have been able to relax more on the mound in game situations, but I still think I will throw harder once I get even more comfortable with my rhythm. I'm able to control each of the five pitches and the movement on my two-seamer is back to where it was years ago.

43

If not for most of the players using metal bats I probably would have broke about five wood bats last game. They had one player use wood and I broke two of his bats, but he managed a weak hit on one of the broken bats."

Emailed October 6:
"I have been talking to some players about your techniques. They have not seen me pitch as smoothly in the past like I have the last two outings. My next game is Sunday in Delaware."

Emailed the following year May 25:
"I managed to throw a complete game shutout the other day. We only play seven innings in these leagues because it gets dark and they have no lights. I struck out nine and gave up three hits while shattering a few wood bats.

But more importantly, the mental game and confidence is there and I am not battling myself. In fact, I am even more relaxed on the mound than ever. I have the feeling that when a situation that normally would cause stress is now comfortable, and I enjoy getting out of these situations. I recall the same feeling when I was a closer in college." --- Chris Mitchell

CHAPTER NINE

REMOVE THE FEAR
LIVE THE DREAM

"Now I see how many guys have it. I never realized before how much of the game is mental. You can see it when guys walk up to the plate, which guys are afraid. I'm sure they could see the fear in my eyes." --- Mike Stanley, former catcher Texas Rangers

Psychotherapists may label what they perceive as players' mental blocks as fears -- fear of failure or fear of success. They may even put psychiatric labels on them. But labels belong best on clothing, not on athletes.

Diagnostically labeling without successfully remedying is another way the invisible opponent even tricks psychologists and psychiatrists to unwittingly add more clutter to a player's mind. And talk-therapies don't address the invisible opponent as the cause and perpetrator of your mysterious mechanics.

There is a widely held belief that "One part of me wants to be successful while another part of me wants to be a failure." But who in their "right mind" wants to be a failure? The truth is that no *part* of you wants anything but you to be successful and achieve your life's goals. It is the invisible opponent that puts you in this inner battle. And so far it has had most of the world believing it is true.

Don't you believe it for even a moment.

Many psychologists and psychiatrists believe they need to have a detailed, personal history and a therapeutic relationship before they can help players begin to resolve their mechanical difficulties. They are convinced that there must be significant emotional events leading up to it. Maybe there was a significant event in his personal life - with his wife or girlfriend, or a business failure. Something that caused a loss of self-esteem, and he started to question himself.

Even if these dynamics do exist, the treating therapist ends up with a player sitting across from him who is not only *not* playing the way he used to, but a player who is being asked to relive his history that may be full of painful memories unrelated to his baffling mechanics in the first place. It just adds more clutter.

Why would one ever try to enlist the logical hemisphere of a player's left, analytical brain when the original problem, the disconnect, entered the illogical hemisphere of his right brain, more precisely, his imagination?

A Japanese expression would explain the rationale for such an approach: "When the only tool one has is a hammer, then the entire world looks like a nail."

All of us have personal issues off the job -- athletes as well. But they don't necessarily result in a player's becoming disconnected from his or her mechanics. One player makes an error and is able to forget about it. Another player makes a bad throw and can't get it out of his head.

There are times, obviously, when psychotherapy is an excellent way of helping athletes work through personal problems off the field. It has proven to be highly successful in dealing with relationship issues, losses, personal growth and childhood issues affecting the quality of one's life.

However, athletes' inexplicable problems are just that -- mysterious and mystifying -- and not psychological.

A much more effective and practical approach is to move out of the analytical mind where the player is already drowning, and walking him over to his imagination where he can materialize and conquer his problems.

IT SHOWS HOW THE MENTAL LEADS THE PHYSICAL

Grant, a 21-year-old college ballplayer, presented a story that on the surface appeared difficult to respond to with so many variables involved. On the surface, it would appear that his situation should possibly have him seeking a psychotherapist.

But since the effects of his problems presented themselves in his mechanics, I was able to stay focused on just those issues. I walked him through the inner landscape of his imagination. He improved in many areas of his life.

I HAVEN'T FELT THIS GOOD IN A LONG, LONG TIME

"My name is Grant Alexander. I'll be attending Washington State next year where I'll be a junior. I wasn't able to play last summer due to my car wreck. I had a minor concussion; my neck and shoulders were stiff for all of the summer and up into September. I was treated with acupressure and that got rid of most of the tension. My health was restored last fall.

I started out hot in the fall. I was hitting everything on the nose. I was also going to be a pitcher, but the car wreck had taken some velocity from my arm as well. I was only throwing 82 when I had the abilities to throw low 90's before my car wreck. All the other positions were filled up. (I mainly play the corners.)

I had a verbal commitment to Oklahoma State University so I wasn't really worried about anything until October-November. I hadn't heard from my recruiting coach since September when I committed.

In early October one of my friend's died in the same type of car accident that I had. It was really a tough time because it could have happened to me.

Then I got the news that OSU wasn't going to sign me.

I came back from the holiday break hitting the ball real well. Our first series I lined out every at bat. I had just a few hits, but everything else was hit right at somebody.

The next week my grandfather (dad's side) passed away. All I could think about was losing my father.

Two weeks later, our assistant coach's wife died. Then all I could think about was losing my mother.

It was all downhill from there. I wasn't playing as much and I didn't know what to do. I still am so scared about losing my family, especially during travel. My spring season didn't turn out very well because I had put so much pressure on myself to show them I really could hit.

I have no trouble seeing the ball and I've tried everything, but nothing seems to work. I don't understand it. I work and practice harder than anyone around me and I know that I'm better than them, but it's just not showing."

I worked with Grant over the telephone and addressed all the issues he presented in his email. The next day I received the following email from him:

"Wow, I can't even begin to start to tell you how great and confident I felt yesterday when I got off the phone with you. All of my friends at the cabin *where I'm staying kept asking what was wrong with me. I just told them I was high on life. It was so weird. It seemed like everything was happening for me.*

I hit the ball really well and it felt like my arm was unlocked or something. This is really weird. I'll keep you posted."

Four days went by and I received an email from a very happy camper:

"I'M BACK!!!!! I haven't felt this good in a long, long time Dr. C. I can't describe the amount of confidence that I have in every aspect of my game and even in life. I even feel like I'm getting more attention from the ladies. I've been feeling like my old self as of late thanks to you. I'll keep you posted."

Six days later:

"I cannot believe how amazing I feel and it's translating into the games. In the past few games I've raised my average, felt more confident in my catching and my arm.

All my hits seem to be coming towards the end of the game. In the past I would have shut it down mentally if I didn't have a good at-bat my first one or two times up. I had a big double the other night in my last at-bat to bring in two runs and I eventually scored to tie it up in the bottom of the ninth.

Everyone on my team says that my swing looks so much better and I carry myself a lot higher than I used to."

And then Grant wrapped it up:

"Things are going well here and I'm really making some progress with everything. Anytime things start going south I just stop and talk to that symbolic imagery. I still can't believe how weird it is. It's so easy and just shows me how much the mental leads the physical. Thanks again." --- Grant Alexander

It is understandably a difficult concept for many professionals, ball players, coaches and organizations to comprehend that struggling athletes can actually use their imagination to return themselves to their previous excellent mechanics. If I hadn't had such immediate and dramatic results over the years, I would find it hard to believe myself.

You may need to suspend what you have believed as *reality* in approaching players' struggles in order to gain a new perspective that can help them reconnect. Its applications go well beyond the arena of sports.

Most therapists and sports psychologists believe that the psychotherapy model used for treating psychological issues applies to struggling players as well. The appropriate model that applies to athletes is Mentalball because it does not approach players or their struggles as psychological in nature. So there is no need to treat them "psychologically," but rather "imaginalogically," if you will.

It goes directly after the manifestations in your mechanics. You do not have to reveal any personal history outside of your sports struggles and how they present themselves. The solution is waiting to be addressed in its own universal language found in the imagination.

TWO HITS AND TEN STRIKEOUTS

Lisa Freihe, a freshman from Doane College, was struggling with her mechanics on the mound. She was well aware that a member of her family and his severe health problem was affecting her when she contacted me:

"When playing positions such as first or third base, my defensive play has been solid. My hitting has been pretty good as well. My problem occurs on the pitching mound where I have control issues. This may come from several different factors.

50

I allowed the three feet increase in distance from the mound to home plate affect more than it should have. The adjustment to the whole college scene may have been a factor. But, the one thing that I think has affected me the most is the fact that my little brother, Scott, was diagnosed a couple of months ago with brain cancer.

Scott and I are very close and being away from the family through this whole thing has been very difficult. I know he is going through a lot right now and I want to be close to him. Even though I don't think about him when I am on the mound, it may be affecting my concentration.

In high school I was the main pitcher and pitched all but three games my senior year. They relied on me and I knew I would always be the one pitching and I had all the confidence in my pitching and I knew my team did too. I don't feel that I have established any of that at the college level."

After we worked on several points introduced by Lisa, I received feedback from her coach, Barry Mosley:

"Dr. Crowley, I just wanted to get you an update on Lisa's progress. We're heading out on a three-day road trip (6 conference games) tomorrow, and Lisa is staying back to be closer to her family in case something would happen.

Due to a minor injury to another pitcher on Tuesday, I put Lisa in. She hadn't practiced much with the team (only two days,) but I told her she could do it, and get in there and just get it done. She pitched one inning against Hastings and after sailing two balls over the catchers head during her warm-ups, she proceeded to strike out the side.

It was great seeing her be successful again. It wasn't their weak hitters either; it was their third, fourth and fifth ones. I gave her a high five as she came off the field and told her that I knew she could do it. I'm so grateful for your generous assistance. She still might not be out of the woods, but she is making progress, that's for sure. To be honest, I was more happy for her success than anything else that happened that night. It was like a happy-ending to a movie. Thanks!" --- Coach Barry Mosley

Next I heard from Lisa:

"I have been doing really well, but there always seems to be at least one inning that I don't do well. It is always in the first couple of innings, and after that I do fine. I feel myself still doubting a couple of pitches while on the mound. It is just certain pitches. But I feel a lot more comfortable after working with you.

And we just received great news with my brother just yesterday. He had an MRI on his brain and what they could tell, there doesn't seem to be any sign of a tumor left. We won't know for sure until later today, but if that is the case then he will start radiation."

We worked some more on her pitching issues and two weeks later I received Lisa's uplifting email:

"I wanted to let you know the good news. We had two games on Saturday. We lost the first game and we won the second. I pitched the game that we won! It felt so good to be in control again. They only had two hits against me and I had 10 strikeouts! I just want to say thanks so much for everything that you have done for me."---Lisa Friehe

CHAPTER TEN

BODY PATTERNS ON THE MOUND
AND AT THE PLATE

"According to Freud and Karl Marx, fantasy is an escape from reality and responsibility. According to Abraham Maslow, fantasy is the means by which a determined man masters reality." --- Colin Wilson

The invisible opponent is your mind's opponent. It gives rise to the mental patterns stored in your body including how you hold your body when playing.

Some players tell me their coaches and teammates clearly notice these different patterns expressed in their body while on the mound and comment: "You looked different!" "Who was that pitching on the mound today? It wasn't you." "Who was that at the plate? Not you. You held your body differently. You moved differently."

SOMETHING JUST CLICKED

Wayne Foltin was a pitcher in his junior year at UNLV. One day he suddenly found himself disconnected from the game he had played effortlessly since a young boy. Just the year before he was predicted to be a top first-rounder. *Something* was holding him back from pitching consistently, especially before starting the third inning:

"Well, where do I start? This past weekend I had another outing like the weekend before. It went well close to the first two innings and then entering the third inning it just feels weird. The seams on the ball seem weird. I start trying to aim the ball. I leave the ball up and in on a righty.

My other problem is fielding a ball. A bunt will be laid down and for whatever reason something goes through my head that makes me fumble with the ball or the throw is off. I also have a thing for pick off, such as to first base. I have this feeling that I could throw it away, so instead I try to avoid picking over.

Well, hopefully this can help you get started on my disease. How soon can we get going?"

It was interesting how Wayne had become indoctrinated with the word disease referring to his bedeviling mechanics. "Cure" can now replace "disease" for any athlete who is open to another approach.

We worked on more of Wayne's presenting issues. His email the following day indicated a shift in his approach that began to re-awakened his previous outstanding mechanics when scouted as a first-round pick:

"I threw last night and this morning. Let's just say when I took the mound in both games my mom said I was like a totally different pitcher. She noticed I held myself differently. She felt relaxed for the first time in a while.

It was like something just clicked when I got in the game. I was relaxed, focused and in the zone. Last night I retired every batter I faced, although I only pitched an inning and 2/3. Today, however, I pitched three full innings. The first two innings went 1, 2, 3.

. The third inning went blooper to right field because I didn't throw my curve low enough. Then I got a ground ball to short and he bobbled the ball so we only got the out at 2nd. Then I walked a guy. Next guy flew out and then the next

guy grounded out to 1st. I felt really good last night. My fastball was fast and my curveball and change-up were on." --- Wayne Foltin

We worked together intermittently using fifteen minute sessions a number of times over a period of several months. In the last six weeks of his season with UNLV his game came full circle. He even got an all-important win against their nemesis, Brigham Young University.

By season's end of his junior year, Wayne was drafted by the San Francisco Giants. He played Class A short-season for the Salem-Keizer Volcanoes and ended the season with 2-1 record and a 3.38 ERA. While his stats were good they didn't reflect how well he pitched and how good he felt about himself.

Statistics don't necessarily paint a complete picture. They can be deceiving at times.

The same story holds true for hitters as it does for pitchers. Their invisible opponent manifests how they hold their bodies at the plate. Sometimes they chase the ball. Sometimes their stance is slightly altered -- their feet are separated differently.

Helpful comments and suggestions from teammates can't penetrate for some reason. Somehow they can't seem to hear what their coaches are saying. Something has blindsided them. Sammy Sosa's conflict with Chicago Cubs' Dusty Baker during the middle of his 2004 season sheds light on Sosa's invisible opponent at work.

The *Daily News'* Tony Jackson described it best: *"Baker's frustration with the former NL MVP began when Sosa inexplicably began standing farther away from the plate in the batter's box, leaving him vulnerable to just about anything over the outside corner."*

Colorado Rockies Todd Helton entered the 2005 season with a .339 career batting average, averaging 35 homers and 118 RBI in each of his first seven full seasons. It certainly made the news when his batting average dropped some 80 points. He only had six homers and 26 RBI on the heels of the first three months of the season.

"I haven't had a consistent approach at anything," said Helton. *"I've changed my stance 42 times in 42 games, and that's basically the result of not trusting yourself, and I have myself to blame for that."*

Rockies' manager Clint Hurdle added, *"I've watched him swing the bat for seven years in this game, and he's swinging as well as I've seen him in the cage and in batting practice. But when the lights come on, he just gets in a hurry again. He's become a bigger enemy than the opposing pitcher, and that's somewhat frustrating."*

So the invisible opponent can infect the best in the business. It conned Helton into believing he was to blame for his stance. It even conned Hurdle into believing Helton was not only his own worst enemy, but the team's as well.

In most cases as time passes, players do come out of their slumps. Helton did. But why wait helplessly for it to end when you can distance yourself from it immediately? As weird as the problem feels to the players, their invisible opponent's hold on them can be released fairly quickly.

When you can see your mistakes, you have a better chance to change them. Similarly, when you can see your invisible opponent at work through the lens of your minds' eye, you can also learn to change its negative influence.

The "shift" in your mind that solves your problem does not take place with words. It does happen by making your invisible opponent's disarming strategies visible through the intentional use of your imagination.

MY MINDSET IS WHERE IT NEEDS TO BE

Michael Gilmartin of Crespi High School in Southern California had a batting average of .466 when his junior year regular season ended. His team did so well, they made it to the playoffs held at Dodger Stadium. However, during the playoffs it was a different story. Michael struck out four times and the fun of playing ball disappeared.

His invisible opponent infected him with negative thinking and pressure and he became separated from his once relaxed and confident manner of approaching the plate. Overanalyzing impacted the way he held himself at the plate as well as his focus on the ball. After an hour of working in person with these problems, I received an email five days later:

"Thank you for all of the help you gave me with my hitting. After two winter league games, I am really starting to feel more confident at the plate. When I am in the box, my head is cleared of clutter and distracting thoughts now.

I also feel that my tension level is decreasing and I am able to see the ball more clearly as well. I am also noticing that I am starting to hit the ball much harder with somewhat effortless swings. In the two games in which I have played, I have only gotten two hits, but I have hit several balls hard.

Since working with you, I have also become more disciplined at the plate. I have laid off a great deal of pitches that were out of the zone that I would used to swing at. This newly acquired discipline has allowed me to get on base more often, which is very important for me because my role on the team at this point is to be a leadoff hitter.

Lastly, I am starting to regain the joy and excitement that I have had when I am playing. Thank you for all of your help! I am also looking forward to meeting and working with you again to help transform my game, and life, to higher levels of success."

Two months later I heard from Michael and we worked with the issues he presented in the following email:

"I am feeling great at the plate when I am hitting left handed. I feel as if I can hit anybody. The problem that I am having on this side of the plate is that I am currently not swinging at pitches I can drive with less than two strikes.

I am getting a good amount of hits, but I am not driving the ball as well as I am capable of doing. When I turn around to hit right handed, I really feel as if I have no confidence. I am swinging late, and I am swinging at bad balls. I am making contact, but the quality of the contact is not crisp and pure."

We worked the next day on Michael's discomfort hitting right-handed, his being somewhat too aggressive and his lack of solid contact. Two weeks later I received his progress report:

"I just wanted to let you know that all is going well at the plate. I am doing a good job of feeling more relaxed, and less tensed up. I now feel that I am playing with less pressure on myself.

By the end of the season Michael had received a baseball scholarship to the University of California at Irvine, a Division One college in the Big West Conference:

"I am doing great. My high school season has been finished for several weeks now due to the fact that we were unable to make it to the playoffs. I had a summer league game last night and went 2-for-3. My mindset right now is where it needs to be. Thanks for all your help."---Michael Gilmartin

CHAPTER ELEVEN

CONSPIRACY OF SILENCE

"Nobody ever told me that other players went through it. They just told me I stunk." --- Former Tigers' third baseman Darnell Coles

Your invisible opponent may convince you to keep your struggles to yourself, which leads to over-thinking, second-guessing and subsequently, more noise in your head. Sometimes you may have conversations with yourself similar to the following:

> *"This is weird. If I tell anybody they'll think I'm weird. They may even make fun of me. They'll view me as being weak, a complainer. I may lose my spot in the rotation. The coach won't let me play if I tell him about the bizarre discomfort in my arm. How can I tell anyone my hand feels strange only in a game, but it's fine in practice? It sounds off the wall so I'll just keep it to myself."*

You have just been talked into a secret, a secret that adds the last thing you need -- more extraneous thoughts. You are convinced that this decision to keep your mouth shut is yours and are completely unaware of how your invisible opponent operates. *It* becomes stronger and more empowered when not discussed, not shared.

Rich McGinnis, like many others, described hiding his personal nightmare:

"I've lived with baseball's dark secret and tried to overcome it in every possible manner all the while trying to hide it from everyone around me. I felt embarrassed about having difficulty making a simple throw...one that anyone can do."

ALMOST QUIT PLAYING BASEBALL

Steve Daeges, a high school coach, contacted me about his son, Zach, who attended Creighton University. All of a sudden Zach's wheels came off and he couldn't throw like he had since he was a kid:

"I was trying to find some solution to my son, Zach's, throwing problems. Zach developed a problem throwing towards the end of the season. He went to Creighton University in Omaha Nebraska as a pitcher, infielder. Last summer he was throwing the ball in the low 90's.

Things were going well until he had a game where he made a few bad throws and all of a sudden it was like he never played before.

I really don't know how to help him. I'm a high school coach and have never dealt with this with any player and now the player who has the problem is my son. I know it is very difficult to solve and really don't know where to turn. It's really hard seeing him go through this." --- Steve Daeges

I spoke with Zach and we worked on many issues, such as his release point, overthinking, tightness in his arm, and fear to let loose and throw hard.

The following outcomes occurred after two and a half hours of work with Zack using Mentalball's approach. It took place during four sessions over a span of a couple of months:

"I've actually been doing really well. Just this last week I threw probably the best bullpen of my life.

And also this week I threw an inning in a scrimmage and I did pretty well. Everything is pretty much back to normal with pitching other than just getting more comfortable on the mound again.

The weird thing is another kid on my team has a similar problem to what I had. He is a pitcher and he is really struggling with it and I let him know about your website and told him to check it out. I'm not sure if he did or not. He thinks that it's getting better now, but I'm not sure if it is or not. I'll have to talk to him this week and see how it's going.

It was funny talking to him though, because he was like, "You wouldn't understand; no one would believe me." I know how it is. It's such a relief not to have to worry about throwing anymore. It was killing me and now everything is good again.

I just want to thank you for everything because I don't know what would have happened if I wouldn't have talked to you. I probably would have quit. But now everything is good. Thanks again." --- Zach Daeges

IT HELPS TO TALK

Talking about your struggles is a most important ingredient in getting out of the hole. Silence encases you. It is like adding water to cement. Tom Haudricourt wrote about this issue that appeared in *Baseball America* August, 2005:

> *The way the 2005 season began for Milwaukee Brewers outfielder, Corey Hart, he began to wonder if he had ever been a good hitter.*
>
> *"I had 11 hits in April," the Triple-A Nashville outfielder said. "That's kind of a big hole to get out of. I tried to stay back and attack the ball. I tried every thing in the book. It got to the point where I almost forget how to swing because I was trying so many different things. You look up and everybody's getting off to a good start and you're hitting below .100. It kind of got to me and I was pressing a little bit."*

After a nightmarish April, when he batted .157 Hart found his stroke in May. He batted. 306, and his resurgence had begun. He went nuts in June, batting .413. Hart said, "You start to wonder, 'What am I doing wrong?' It was just a matter of getting my confidence back."

Hart said he kept his sanity during the dark days by communicating with buddy J. J. Hardy, who had a tough first half offensively as a rookie shortstop in Milwaukee. "It helped to talk," Hart said. "We were both going through the same thing. You just keep working and swinging and try to get out of it."

The moment players becomes aware of it, they need to discuss it with their friends, family and coaches so they can seek an immediate remedy. Also, coaches need to be on the lookout for this phenomena so they can sit the player down, discuss it and find help. There is no reason for any player to lose his or her dream.

THE MONKEY IS OFF MY BACK

Matt Midkiff believed his inability to throw was unique to him. However, it is more pervasive than most people are aware or willing to admit. Former Fresno State University Hall of Fame coach Bob Bennett referred to it as *"an endemic problem in all sports, not just baseball."* Matt wrote:

"I was amazed to find that I wasn't the only one who had these issues when I went to your site. I am one year into my baseball coaching career and have lost the ability to throw. It seemed like all of a sudden I just couldn't throw strikes. Then it turned into not even being able to play catch.

I know it's a mental problem because when I throw against a wall or net I am fine. This problem has me thinking I will never be able to become a top level coach because I can't throw BP.

I just completed my Master's Degree at Wilkes University in PA where I was a gradate assistant. I have applied for some assistant jobs and am hoping to get some info back soon. I do want to clear up this problem first though so I can be confident in all aspects of coaching. Any help you could provide would be great."

Matt and I worked within his imagination. He, like every player I've worked with, literally and figuratively *imagined* his way out of his throwing problem:

"I am so relieved that with your help I have taken the first step to getting over this problem. I had a chance to throw today and I was simply amazed. I was a little tentative at first, but once I relaxed things seemed to flow like they haven't in a long time. The short throws were crisp and on target. I threw again several more times and felt really good.

The monkey is off my back! Thank you so much"

One month later:

"I did get a call a couple weeks ago about a job in Texas. I had a phone interview and they called me back an hour later to offer me the job. I am now at Frank Phillips College in Borger, Texas. I am the full-time assistant coach and I am absolutely thrilled. It isn't often that you can call somebody a miracle worker, but I owe my career and my future in coaching baseball to you."
--- Matt Midkiff

The conspiracy of silence is not just limited to baseball players. One independent league pitcher told me that he had been struggling for about three weeks. He finally approached the team's manager for help. The manager replied, "Of course I've seen you struggling. I didn't say anything because I didn't want to bring more attention to it and make it worse."

So the invisible opponent is able to generate a conspiracy of silence on both sides, and rationalize its existence.

Mentalball encourages you to speak freely of your experience with friends and other athletes as exemplified in the sharing of stories by players and coaches throughout this book. It is no longer cloaked in the secrecy of the past as being a stigma for a ball player to seek whatever form of mental mechanics coaching that may help.

Yours is not a "mental case," but rather a prank of your imagination -- a very human condition we all experience. Begin to see the root of your problem as being "imagin-al," rather than "ment-al." It takes you out of the equation of being the responsible party for your mechanics that make no sense.

Unfortunately, the mistaken belief of being perceived as weak by yourself or others to request outside help has painted many an athlete into a corner for fear of being ridiculed by teammates or losing his position.

If you think *you* are in control when being silent, think again. It is the invisible opponent orchestrating this fear that keeps you stuck and not progressing with your dreams and career. A number of players' arms and shoulders have sadly been the recipients of "surgery from silence."

Remember, it's a new age. You're a new generation. And there is a new approach.

CHAPTER TWELVE

REMOVE THE CLUTTER
QUIET YOUR MIND

"I'm firmly convinced that one of the biggest difficulties in cases of control problems is that too many suggestions, ideas, theories, etc. can cause clutter. In my mind, clutter is the worst part of the problem." --- Steve Blass

During the latter part of the '70's as catcher with the Atlanta Braves, Dale Murphy recalled, *"Your mind won't let your natural abilities flow. Your mind interferes, and you start thinking, Where am I throwing? What am I doing? Instead of just throwing. Your mind starts working against you."*

It's not *your* mind working against you. Those thought-forms are emanating from your imagination. More specifically, it's your invisible opponent *making* your mind work against you. It leaves you believing that you are the one doing it to yourself. And that leads you to being hard on yourself.

Former New York Yankees catcher Fran Healy said, *"The easiest thing a catcher has to do is throw the ball to the pitcher. It's a thing that should be as easy as opening a door. But having to think about something that simple makes it a problem."*

Some authorities contend players' problems are the result of their consciousness getting in their way. For example, if a musician starts worrying about where his fingers go while he's playing his instrument, it will change the performance.

So how do you circumvent what gets into your consciousness? How do you outwit worrisome thoughts? Thoughts that cause changes in your velocity and delivery? Thoughts that cause you to feel tension and tightness?

While you have no control over thoughts entering your mind, there is a way you can remove and annihilate them.

The St. Louis Cardinals assumed pitcher Rick Ankiel's troubles were mechanical. They said he often rushed his delivery and as a result varied his release point on some throws. Nevertheless, Cardinals pitching coach, Dave Duncan, conceded the problem also might be mental: *"In the end, the problem is mechanics. It's something that leads to that. It's probably thoughts that lead to that."*

People in baseball refer those thoughts as the "little man," an imaginary person sitting on the shoulder of a player. Former Florida Marlins manager John Boles said in 2001 that there is not much at all that coaches or players --or even psychiatrists for that matter --can do to get rid of him:

> *"No one knows why it shows up, and it leaves when it wants. It's a demon. It's strictly in the mind, and I have seen some doozies. I have seen a lot of catchers who can't throw the ball back to the pitcher. I have seen staff members who couldn't throw batting practice. The little man has a mind of his own. He sits right here on your shoulder and talks to you. He's whispering in your ear. Gets in your head when you're throwing. And you can't believe -- baseballs go up, down, inside, outside, all over the place."*

When Mark Mulder was with the Oakland Athletics, he posted great numbers. He lead the American league with 21 wins in 2001 and compiled ERAs below 3.50 each season from 2001-2003

By the time he began the 2004 All-Star Game for the American League he had a record of 12-2. However, during the second half of 2004 he was no longer calling his pitches, his invisible opponent was. Mulder said, *"I started thinking too much down the stretch."*

Mulder conceded he lost the form during his 2005 season he had from 2001 through 2003: *"There hasn't been a single game this season that I've left and thought I'd thrown the way I did two or three years ago."* Cardinals pitching coach Dave Duncan commented on Mulder:

> *"He's doing a lot of things differently. His delivery is a lot longer than it used to be and it's taking him a long time to correct it. How it happened, I don't know. It probably happened over the course of the past couple years. He's developed some bad habits and it's hard to get out of them...He knows it. He sees it. He feels it. But in the heat of battle, it's harder to make adjustments."*

How do you develop bad habits? Where do they come from? And why is it so hard to get out of them? Knowing you have them, why can't you break out of them? Especially in Mulder's case where "He knows it. He see it. He feels it."

Once again it was Mulder's invisible opponent waging the battle with him. It convinced Mulder, his coaches, reporters and fans that he was the one completely responsible for overcoming his baffling mechanics.

Yet, your invisible opponent can be obliterated, and with it, bad habits.

I'M ABLE TO CLEAR EVERYTHING OUT

Anthony Del Grosso, a left-handed pitcher from New Jersey, had just about given up all hope of ever pitching like he did in the past. His following email told it all:

"I need help! Next year I will be a senior at a Division ll college. I am a 21-year-old, 6' 3", 220 lb LHP who has seemed to have forgotten how to throw the ball. I work my butt off and can do it in practice when it's just me and the catcher…no coaches. In the game it's a different story.

I am currently being scouted by numerous teams. In my last successful outing I was by far my best. I struck out three out of four hitters I faced with my fast ball touching 90 plus mph and my curve falling off the table. After that I began talking to a lot of scouts and former players.

Ever since then I can not find that comfort zone. I have read books about anxiety problems and all types of mental things, but cannot find a cure. It seems that after every good day, a horrible day will follow.

I throw heat and spots in the bullpen and I'm smooth. But during a game I can't remember my name. One day I'm OK, the next day I'm awful. It's like I'm afraid of success. Right after my best outing the beginning of the season my confidence took a nose dive."

I had Anthony confront the invisible opponent in his imagination that he told me was making him squeeze the ball too tightly when he'd throw it. We went after his robotic-like movement that occurs when he finds himself thinking about it. Then we dealt with his confidence issues and his fear of success. The next day he emailed me some of the results:

"I threw last night and I had great control for two and 1/3 innings of work. I felt pretty good. I was focused and hit my spots good. I saw the minimum of six batters and I got the six of them out in a row! I was focused like in the past and I felt good, but I was concentrating on staying clear and was a little afraid to cut it loose, but my velocity was good… around 86-88.

I had good command of it. Thanks for the help so far. Every time I had a second thought about a pitch I was able to use your technique and reminded myself that I had killed that thought already."

We worked on another matter of the ball hitting the back stop which was a problem too. It went well:

"The tryouts went extremely well. I threw hard and hit my spots. It was probably the best I have ever throw -- control-wise.

Oh, and another thing, during the tryout I was able to cut it loose and throw strikes. It felt great! And I was completely calm -- even with everyone there watching. I just need to develop consistency in my thought patterns. I still have a little hesitation that I need to get rid of. Other then that, I feel <u>much</u> better."

Anthony summarized his past month's playing:

"I'm playing pretty good. I'm able to clear everything out. I threw the other day in relief for my team and finally threw strikes and got the win. The more I throw, whether it's good or bad, I feel that I am getting mentally stronger. Thanks for the help."---Anthony Del Grosso

Players are afraid of their "thinking-demons" that lurk in the shadows of downtime and interfere with their focus. However, there is a way to neutralize downtime and worrisome thought and quiet their mind.

The mental component boils down to first, acknowledging the existence of your invisible opponent; and secondly, to conquer its contrary influence and replace it with a mindset that makes you play relaxed, confident and consistent. As strange as the problem feels to a player, the invisible opponent's hold can be released quickly.

FOCUSED, AGGRESSIVE AND CONFIDENT ATTITUDE.

Ben Colton contacted me to resolve the grip his invisible opponent had on his overanalyzing and overthinking. The more he tried to understand his issues, the more entangled he found himself. Transforming his overthinking into images allowed him to dismantle his invisible opponent and retrieve his mechanics:

"I am a sophomore at a junior college in Northern California. I am a 6'5'' 225 lbs pitcher and was a draft and follow for a major league team.

After recovering from a head injury I had the most innings and lowest ERA of the returning staff. My Goal is to be a starting pitcher this year. My problem is that I overanalyze and overthink everything. I am not happy being at a junior college; because I love school I miss the stimulation of the university classroom. My negative attitude towards Juco and my wondering if I should have gone to a Division One school reflects on the field.

My dad, currently a scout within MLB, played minor league ball and has always stressed mechanics. So I overthink and drive myself crazy over having to have perfect mechanics. I go into a game and think about my mechanics and less about the pitch. I also have a "fake confidence" on the mound. I need to become confident realistically. I would be very grateful if you could help me out."

I used my Mentalball approach with Ben on October 16. We targeted several symbolic images he came up with including the ones that had him thinking that he had to be perfect to get the starting position.

We also focused on the symbolic images to resolve his negative attitude regarding not being in the school he desired, overthinking and overanalyzing to have perfect mechanics, and what he termed as "fake confidence" on the mound. I received the following results a week later:

"I pitched Friday with a focused, aggressive and confident attitude. My scout was even out there from a major league organization and I remained locked in. I look forward to our next session!"

October 26 I emailed Ben to let me know what else had shifted in his mechanics and attitude since we did the work. He emailed me his mini-progress reports:

Emailed November 1:
   "I had my best outing of the year Friday the 29th!

Emailed November 11:
   "Things have been going Fantastic! I have pitched great the last four weeks in a row. I have not let up a run since I first talked to you on the phone."

Emailed February 25:
   "I am doing fantastic. I am the number two starter with a 1-0 record so far. I pitched well against USF although it was a scrimmage. I am starting this Saturday against American River."

Emailed March 8:
   "I went eight and pitched a gem against a top team in Northern California. Thanks for all your help." --- Ben Collins

OVERCOMING SEROUS SETBACKS

Skip Wood's article in *USA TODAY* June 30, 2005 showed how Roy Halladay, American League Cy Young winner in '03 with the Toronto Blue Jays, overcame some serious setbacks. *"No longer are flaws in his delivery hidden nor self-described "demons" in his head."* He did it with the assistance of an unorthodox approach by pitching coach Mel Queen who rebuilt his mechanics.

Queen said, *"Even though he threw hard, they hit him because they saw the ball so good. It was straight as an arrow. So I completely redid everything he did, just took the old guy and buried him and created something new."*

What Queen describes he did as a pitching mechanics coach for Halladay parallels the Mentalball approach using mental mechanics coaching. Queen "buried the old guy" and "created something new." Mentalball dismantles the symbolic representation of the invisible opponent and returns players to their original mechanics anew.

When working with subtle energies, players sometimes describe having the equivalence of amnesia for ever having had the problem when it is finally behind them. It is as if it never happed to them. It is more like something they have seen in a movie or read about. They become that far removed from their struggles.

Tampa Bay Devil Rays' pitcher Barrett Wright describes his "amnesia" for his previous wild throwing off the mound: *"After my throwing problem ended, it was as though I had never had it in the first place. I can't explain it any more than that. It just left me."*

The difference between Queen's approach and Mentalball is found in Halladay's comment alerting you that his invisible opponent is gone, but not forgotten. Halladay said, *"You always have these thoughts creeping into your head, a picture, of how things might not work out. That's the biggest challenge sometimes, getting rid of those mental pictures and putting positive things in there. If you can get away from that and avoid that, in any part of your life, it makes a huge difference."*

The combination of coaching and Mentalball can make a huge difference too.

CHAPTER THIRTEEN

JUDGMENT VS COMPASSION

"I never blame myself when I'm not hitting. I just blame the bat and if it keeps up, I change bats. After all, if I know it isn't my fault that I'm not hitting, how can I get mad at myself?" --- Yogi Berra

If it is not your purposeful intention for problematic experiences to happen to you, then don't sit in judgment on yourself. Being angry and frustrated with yourself reawakens painful and punitive memories, the last thing you want while playing your game.

Self-directed anger can become the breeding grounds of a psychic virus unleashing your invisible opponent. It may obstruct or even preclude the healing, the reconnecting of your mechanics from taking place.

The word heal comes from the root "hale" or "whole" and to heal means to make whole. When your mechanics are reconnected you are whole, at one with yourself in body-mind-spirit.

Being compassionate, even if you have to act "as if" you're compassionate with yourself, is the medicine you need to restore your lost mechanics, not the prescription of blame and shame.

The trickster generating this false belief is your invisible opponent. It is the troublemaker. It is the mastermind sitting in the shadows

instigating your internal fight -- making you believe that the battle is of your own doing.

I NO LONGER BEAT MYSELF UP

Matt Goliber, a sophomore catcher from Creighton University, was consumed with negative thoughts and fear of failure:

"I would like to be able to get back to the point where I can play ball without having the fear to fail in my head. The point where the negative thoughts don't consume me and prohibit me from doing normal things like catching the ball and making it pop when it hits my catcher's mitt or throwing the ball back to the pitcher.

I catch at Creighton University and am stuck in the bullpen right now because of these setbacks. I'm looking forward to enjoying this game again, and any help you can give me in accomplishing this goal."

I spoke with Matt and walked him through the process of Mentalball. We worked on his fear of not catching a ball, his struggle receiving it and the strange experience of how the ball pops when it hits his mitt. I heard back about a month later:

"Things have been going much better in the bullpen. My coach had a meeting with each of us a couple weeks ago and said the scrimmage that I had before I talked to you basically made him decide that I wouldn't play the rest of the year. So I can't say how it is on the field. I have been warming up pitchers in between innings on the field and that has been going well. I'll send you an email after summer ball starts and let you know how it is going on the field."

P.S. I did get a chance to pinch hit late in one game a few weeks ago and I felt confident and in control, so that was positive.
. P.P.S. Buck said that you have helped him look at doing something wrong as not such a big deal and that has definitely been a feeling I've felt. Before when I would drop a ball I would beat myself up, now I just think "screw it."

Five months later Matt got back to me:

"Summer ball went really well as I thought it would, but what was a pleasant surprise was that fall ball also went well back here at Creighton. The two catchers in front of me outplayed me so I was once again stuck back in the bullpen, but at least it was because of talent reasons and not mental reasons."
--- Matt Goliber

CHAPTER FOURTEEN

FULL BLOWN SLUMP

"You can't depend on your eyes when your imagination is out of focus."
--- Mark Twain

Reporter Jim Souhan wrote an insightful article depicting a player with a gun to his head by his invisible opponent. It appeared in the *Minneapolis Star Tribune* June 27, 2004 entitled "Hitting slump consumes Doug Mientkiewicz." I've interspersed observations throughout it:

When Doug Mientkiewicz slumps, he sees the ball, all right. He sees a pea-sized leather-seeking hummingbird whose elusiveness cramps his career, income, sleep, relationships and mental health.

"It's driving me nuts," he said.

Mientkiewicz settles for mood swings. "My slumps affect everybody," he said. "My mom, my dad, my friends, my wife. I wake up, it's the first thing in my head. It woke me up at 7 a.m. today. You feel like it's the last day of summer and school's starting tomorrow."

Mientkiewicz has batted .300 two of the past three years. [In 2003] he finished ninth in the American League in on-base percentage, yet [halfway through the 2004 season] his average is hovering around .240 and his head is spinning like a Pedro Martinez curveball.

"I come to the plate and see .240, and I want to puke," he said. "You want to block it out, but you can't. [His wife] Jodi tries to help. One day she's supportive, the next she's jumping me, saying, 'Where's the guy who said he wasn't going to settle for this?'"

The guy who said he wasn't going to settle for this is not the same guy who shows up at the plate. The Mientkiewicz in the batter's box is truly beside himself, disconnected. And his low numbers are evidence of his invisible opponent having a field day with him.

"The game is wrapped so tightly around my brain that when I go through this, I can barely function."

Jodi is so used to the warning signs that she identifies its stages.

"The first part is always the 0-for-10," she said in an email. "It might only be a two-or three-day period with no hits or bad luck but it is the sure sign that a slump is on the way. Kind of like an itchy throat telling you, here comes a cold. During this time, Doug gets a little frustrated. He comes home and we replay each at-bat but there is still that belief that he will get two hits tomorrow."

"The next phase is the 1-or-2-for-10. . . . The average is dropping noticeably and the frustration has turned to anxiety. Doug starts to doubt himself. He loses confidence."

Doug's invisible opponent has him down on the mat and the count has begun. The invisible opponent makes Doug doubt himself, increases his anxiety and drains his confidence like a vampire with its victim.

[Jodi said,] "He remarks that he doesn't want to be an average player. He gets mad at himself for not contributing. You are officially in the slump and he starts to press to get out of it. This is the time when he will make changes in his stance, in his swing, in his pitch selection.

This is the time that it is hardest to live with him. . . . All the things you have confidence in -- your ability, your eye, your judgment, somehow they all get lost in that 15-foot journey [to the plate]. There are many times when I watch him on TV that I can tell whether or not he is going to get a hit just by looking at his body language."

The shift in the way Doug holds his body is another red flag for the presence of his invisible opponent. It makes him literally forget his natural swing and stance that lead to a batting average of .306 in 2001 and .300 in 2003.

And when he breaks out?

"That is when he begins to open up again," Jodi said. "The irony about all of his slumps is that he always believes the one he is in is the worst of his career."

Bullpen coach Rick Stelmaszek, who's been in pro ball longer than Mientkiewicz has been alive, says he's never seen anybody so hyperanalytical.

"The guys who are good and consistently put up big numbers have convinced themselves that they're good ballplayers," Stelmaszek said. "When you start worrying about everything, you're in self-destruct mode."

Every day Mientkiewicz hears voices in his head. Most belong to him.

The voices that aren't his are those of his invisible opponent taunting Doug with his worst fears. So far they are very convincing.

Worries beget mechanical flaws. A coach, a former player and a scout all offered the same assessments this week, saying Mientkiewicz's right shoulder and hip are "flying open," that he's rolling his weight too quickly to the outside of his right foot, that he's dipping his left shoulder."

But what was it that preceded the "worries [that] beget mechanical flaws?" It was the *point of entry* for Doug's invisible opponent that

disconnected him in the first place. And *then* the worries bubbled up and manifested in his mechanical flaws.

Struggles with his mechanics may be resolved through coaching, suggestions and observations. Or going behind the scenes where his invisible opponent resides and nailing it.

When Mientkiewicz is at his best, he keeps his weight back and uses the whole field. When he slumps, he commits early and pulls hittable pitches foul.

If only Mientkiewicz would read his résumé instead of the scoreboard. He's the best-fielding first baseman in the game. He's won a Gold Glove and an Olympic gold medal. He's hit .300 twice and won two division titles, yet all he can see is his latest line drive finding leather.

"I try to tell myself, 'We're in first place and my team hasn't even needed me; I'll be ready when they do,'" he said. "It's hard not to beat yourself up."

And yet it is easy to fix once you realize you are not the one beating yourself up....although Mientkiewicz was paralyzed by that belief, like many others.

He used to play with a chip on his shoulder; now he's carrying Gibraltar on his back.

"I check the mail once a year at home," he said. "The one time I checked it this year, there was the Sports Illustrated with Derek Jeter on the cover and the title 'Slump' written in big letters."

"Great timing. Thanks."

He may trade in SI for a Psychology Today.

"My average stinks," he said. "My homers stink. My RBI are horrible. And when you get people on base, you feel pressure. It's like the end of the world."

"[Los Angeles Dodgers first baseman/outfielder] Shawn Green was going through this [in 2003 and 2004] and said the more the fans boo him the more it consumes him. That's so true."

In Milwaukee, Mientkiewicz told Gardenhire and GM Terry Ryan he was having the worst year of his career. "They both said, 'You'll be fine,'" Mientkiewicz said. "They're showing confidence in me -- why can't I show it in myself?"

History offers Mientkiewicz hope. [In 2003] he hit .227 in April and finished at .300. His career average in August is .302. "I wake up every morning saying, 'Today's the day,'" Mientkiewicz said.

If this slump were a stalker, at least Mientkiewicz could call the cops. "This, you can't get away from," he said. "This follows you everywhere."

The invisible opponent is indeed a stalker. It ends its stalking when it decides. Or it is ended when you dismantle it. You can overcome its grip the moment it rears its ugly head and avoid falling into a slump altogether.

Mientkiewicz' worst nightmare came true. After being traded to the Boston Red Sox he ended his 2004 season with a batting average of .238. Then he was traded to the New York Mets where he ended his 2005 season hitting .240.

Mientkiewicz is not alone. He is one of many who could benefit from dismantling his invisible opponent that makes players obsess about statistics, and just about everything else.

CHAPTER FIFTEEN

DUMP YOUR SLUMP

"To adhere to an outmoded belief system is like still carrying the raft after you've crossed the river." --- Buddhist saying

When you are in a slump, it is like reading a book only to discover you haven't absorbed a word on the page.

You read it again and find out that your mind has drifted. You see the words. You may even hear yourself thinking while reading the words, but for some reason you are not fully present.

It's as if you are in two places at the same time. Beside yourself. Splintered. Separated from the task at hand. Disconnected.

While more thoughts and analysis can often exacerbate your slump, you do have the option to change them by using your imagination.

I CAN SEE THE STRIKE ZONE

Many times parents and coaches will go online looking for solutions to help their sons and daughters when all else has failed. One such parent was Tina Trimbath who presented her concerns about her son, Tyler:

"I came upon your website and was amazed at what I read about mental mechanics. You describe my son to a T. He has talent and ability, but he has a problem with mental mechanics.

Do you have any suggestions on how to help him overcome his doubts and lack of self confidence. He played college ball and now is playing in an amateur league for 19-20 year-olds. It seems as he has grown older and expectations have become higher, he mentally hurts himself in the game. Your advice would be greatly appreciated." --- Tina Trimbath

Tyler emailed me two days later describing his predicament at the plate:

"My main problem is in the batter's box. I am having problems finding the release point. Balls look like strikes and strikes look like balls.

Before I even get to the plate I get nervous. I have fears of striking out, and once I do strike out I get so mad that I'm pretty much done for the rest of the game. I hate doing badly, mainly because my father and grandfather come to every game. I feel the need to go 3-for-3 or 4-for-4. If I don't, I feel like I let them down.

My coach doesn't help the situation either. He can't stand when I swing at balls and not strikes. I am a Four hitter. I feel pressured to bring in runs. This has been a problem for years now. When I have a coach who expects a lot out of me, I choke."

I worked with the exact words Tyler described in his email as well as what he told me when we spoke on the phone. Contained in each player's word-description of his problem are the underlying, imbedded symbolic images that awaken, like a sleeping giant, usually when he or she enters a game.

Having a player translate his problems into symbolic images through his imagination's innate ability to *pretend,* **allows him to unlock the grip his invisible opponent has held on him. A few days later Tyler contacted me:**

"I wanted to let you know that my practice went well after we spoke.

I had a game every night this week. During my game on Tuesday I did not do so well. I struck out my first two times, singled my third and grounded out my fourth. This is not too bad. I was just glad to hit the ball. The kid that we faced was drafted by the Indians. He was above average. He was a lefty throwing low 90's with a tight slider.

My game on Thursday went better. I saw the ball a little more clearly. I had a single and two ground ball outs. I still think there is a problem though, but it is slowly getting better. However, I would like to talk to you another time."

I worked with Tyler again and he forwarded me his results:

"Things seem to be going better and my mind seems clearer. I am more focused, relaxed and comfortable. I can see the strike zone. I had a double-header and it went very well. I had a hit in each of my games. I believe that what you did with me has helped. Thank you again." --- Tyler Trimbath

CHAPTER SIXTEEN

WELL-MEANING ADVICE
MAY MISS ITS TARGET

"Symbols have the capacity to touch us not just on an intellectual level, but on behavioral and emotional levels as well." --- Albert Einstein

Sometimes you can see the invisible opponent toying with a player for only a few innings, maybe the entire game. Other times it spills over into several games, even into severe struggles and slumps.

When velocity suddenly drops or errant throws suddenly occur, you may want to rule out a physical stress present or an injury in the making that may not be full blown until some time down the road.

Case in point is Detroit Tigers pitcher Nate Cornejo. Within the first month of the 2004 season opposing teams had roughed him up for a 1-3 with an 8.42 ERA, for a league-high .375 batting average. Conejo had allowed 42 hits in 25 innings with 11 walks and 12 strikeouts. *"I'm struggling so much,"* Cornejo said, *"and I don't think my velocity is there, and I'm not letting it all go."*

Cornejo no longer pitched in the major leagues after May 5 2004. By the end of July he underwent season-ending surgery to repair the frayed labrum in his right shoulder. He spent the 2005 season with the Tigers' Double-A Erie Seawolves posting a 4.59 ERA.

Other than a physical problem, the minute a player's fielding, pitching, throwing, catching or hitting *suddenly* drops off, it may be just part of the ebb and flow of playing the game. Or, it may be a signal to get your attention and address it.

Do you panic? Of course not.

Do you pay more attention? Most definitely. View it as a player having a slight fever. The sooner you remedy the first sign of a slump, the better.

Most well-meaning advice for players in slumps is peppered with comments such as: "Be positive." "Focus." "Relax." "Don't think about it." None of which tends to help the player when the invisible opponent is operating.

When former manager of the Tampa Bay Devil Rays' Lou Piniella saw his players struggling at the plate that's when he told them, *"Guys, look, your wife is still going to be there when you get home, your dog will still like you, and you'll still drive the same car. Just relax and hit the ball."*

However, the player is well aware that for some unknown reason he has become separated from his ability to obliterate the worry and be positive, relaxed, and focused.

Sometimes well-intended, yet bombarding advice, not only frustrates players all the more, but it makes them believe that nobody understands what is really going on inside them. They find it very difficult, in not impossible, to put their perplexing situation into words.

When former Texas Rangers pitcher Monty Fariss was struggling he said, *"Everyone wants to help solve the problem, or help create one."* He believed the most frustrating advice to offer any player going through a mental block was to tell him *"not to think"* about it. Former Los Angeles

Dodgers infielder Steve Sax agreed: *"It's like a big elephant in front of you. You can't ignore it."*

How many remember as a child playing word-games with your family or friends to pass the time? You would tell them that the name of the game was to think of anything *but* pink elephants. "Don't think about pink elephants no matter what you do."

However, the mind has a blind spot for the word "don't." It is as if it can't hear that word, but holds onto all the other words. As a result everybody found themselves not only thinking of pink elephants, but seeing images of them as well.

So too, your worrisome thoughts get transformed into images that easily. However, your imagination can transform them back into positive thoughts and accompanying images that will make your body and mind act in unison.

I THREW BULLETS RIGHT AT THE CHEST

A young high school catcher contacted me as he was also frustrated like Sax and Fariss with similar advice:

"My name is Matt Chmura. I am 17-years-old and a senior in high school. I am the catcher on our baseball team. Last year I was defensive player of the year.

Over the summer, for some reason, I had trouble returning the ball to the pitcher. I wouldn't have trouble throwing to second base if a runner were stealing, though.

It seems like I get so nervous before I throw the ball back to the pitcher that I think I'm going to throw it away or throw it badly with everyone watching. People told me, "Don't think about it." I tried thinking of something else while catching, but it doesn't work.

I am extremely worried about this and I have two games a week for the next two months. So as soon as you can help me, I would appreciate it. Thank you."

I worked with Matt over the telephone. We initially dealt with his fear of throwing the ball and his thinking too much about the entire thing. He emailed me his results the day after we worked together:

"I felt good warming up and I threw good warming up. However, I still had some nerves, but nothing as big as how it was! Game time came and I was warming up the pitcher. I threw well. But as I made a warm-up toss down to 2nd, I hurt my elbow and so I didn't catch past the first inning.

The next day I warmed up and I felt good. I felt good after our conversation. I was more confident. I threw on the side fine. But when a batter is in the box, I get nervous. I especially find myself nervous playing in front of people watching.

We worked on his being nervous when a batter is in the box and while playing in front of people. A week later Matt emailed me his experience:

"Hey, well I feel almost 100 percent comfortable, but I still have small troubles. I'm not worried about the crowd or people anymore. It's more about a worry of the ball slipping out of my hand. I think it's some mechanics also. However, I don't have this problem while warming up, just during the game. My trainer doesn't want me to play for at least five days because my elbow needs a rest."

After his elbow healed a few weeks later, we worked on his release point. I told him that the ball slipping out of his hand only *appeared* to be a mechanics issue. If it were just mechanics, then Matt would have been experiencing the same problem both warming up *and* in games:

"Great news! I threw warming up the pitcher in front of everyone. And I threw bullets. Perfect ones. Right at the chest. I felt great."

Later Matt summarized his season:

"The season is over for our team. I have good news and bad news. The bad news is that I tore a tendon in my elbow, so I am out for a few weeks. The good news is that I won the team MVP and got All-League Honors. Also I was selected to play in the All-Star game later in June." --- Matt Chmura

CHAPTER SEVENTEEN

TARGET THE INVISIBLE OPPONENT
NOT THE MECHANICS

"What is now proved was once only imagined." --- William Blake

Your original natural mechanics are still alive and well during the midst of your worst struggles. They are completely intact.

A slump is not about mechanics, *per se*, even though it presents itself in them. So never give up hope.

This paradox appears in the news all the time -- a professional ball player's knowing exactly what his problem is and what he needs to do -- yet continues struggling. Milwaukee Brewers' outfielder Carlos Lee was emerging from a slump early in the 2005 season.

Hitting coach Butch Wynegar said that Lee was *"pulling off the ball"* and trying to lift fly balls rather than driving pitches into the gaps. That, in addition to chasing sliders in the dirt, prompted the slump. *"He knows what he's doing wrong,"* Wynegar said. *"He just hasn't been able to stop."*

Then-Los Angeles Dodgers third baseman Adrian Beltre was a notoriously slow starter. However, during the 2004 season, he never really struggled. By mid-season, he raised his average to .323, with 19 home runs and 52 RBI. Beltre couldn't have put it better on this subject when he said, *"When you start the season good, it makes you a much more confident hitter. **When you're struggling, you try to change little things that you probably shouldn't change**, and you think too much before you go to home plate."*

You don't have to be held captive by your invisible opponent. Change the struggle by acknowledging its role, dismantle it, and the mechanics will automatically fall back in place.

When New York Yankees shortstop Derek Jeter was experiencing a slump that plagued him the beginning in the 2004 season, he admitted to *"jumping at the ball."* *"You're trying so hard to get hits instead of just hitting the ball,"* Jeter says. *"But you can't guide the ball. Your eyes are the key. When your head moves, your eyes move, and you don't see the pitch as long. That's why when you're going good, the ball looks slower."*

When he finally ended the slump, Jeter said, *"It's like a bad dream is over."*

Since dreams take place in your imagination, that is where you would go to reclaim whatever's lost. Change the landscape of your dreams and you change your mechanics. You can definitely end any of your living nightmares.

DREAM YOUR PROBLEMS AWAY

Rich McGinnis conquered his chronic issues that spilled over from "the reality" of his night-dreams into "the reality" of his mechanics:

"I've had a reoccurring dream since I was about 12-years-old. It was more frequent then, but I still have it from time to time as I've gotten older. In the dream I'd be on the mound and would go to throw the ball, but I couldn't release the ball. I'd wake up feeling anxious, but would be quickly reassured that it was just a dream....until my junior year when my dream became a reality.

Within days after working with Dr. Crowley to overcome the monster, I became aware of a profound change in the dreams that had haunted me for years. I was actually throwing free and easy in my dreams. I can't remember ever having a dream in which I was doing that.

The dream's entire landscape changed from a dark, tense background into a bright, relaxed atmosphere where I was throwing free and easy...and having fun. Once more baseball has become fun for me. And once again I'm excited about it!"--- Rich McGinnis

CAN'T WAIT TO GET INTO CLUTCH SITUATIONS

Cindy Eadie, a Canadian Olympic softball player, found herself bewildered and frustrated, having lost her position with the Canadian National Team because of her struggles at the plate. Like Jeter, Cindy experienced a living nightmare, but for a much longer period of time and paid a bigger price tag for it:

"I started playing competitive softball when I was eight-years-old, but it wasn't until I was thirteen that I started to take it really seriously. Softball and, more specifically, hitting, always came naturally to me.

When I recall some games from the past, I can actually see myself getting into the batter's box with confidence and swinging effortlessly at pitches I chose carefully.

I started playing for the Canadian National Team when I was 19-years-old and I found that when I faced some of the most dominant pitchers in the world I began feeling doubtful and anxious at the plate. It didn't take long before I experienced the same feelings even when I faced mediocre pitching at the international level.

These feelings held me back from performing at the level I was capable of and I ultimately self-destructed. My confidence at the plate was extremely low

heading into the summer of 2004 when I competed in a little event called the Olympic Games!

I had tried everything and nothing had been successful to break this year along slump. It wasn't exactly a great time to be hand-cuffed by a fear of failure that came only from a little voice inside my head which I now refer to as my demon."

Cindy's response was astounding. Just like the turtle she was right-side-up after a one-time session over the phone. She played a double-header that very day. This was her response:

"We played two games today and I felt great at the plate.

I went 2-for-3 in the first game and I went 1-for-4 in the second game with one of my outs being a line drive. The line drive was in the bottom of the seventh with bases loaded and two out. The girl caught the ball and we didn't win, but I didn't feel anxious or like I wouldn't get it done. I wasn't doubtful today so that was great.

The shift I have noticed lies in my feeling at the plate. For the past while I have been so anxious/nervous while on deck that I almost dreaded my at bat. Now I can't wait to get into the box in clutch situations.

I went 3-for-4 with two RBI in this morning's game against a US club team from Illinois, and I went 2-for-4 against China tonight.

We beat them 3-to-2 in extra innings and I also got two RBI -- the tying run in the sixth and the winning run in the ninth! So I guess you could say that things are going pretty well!

I wish I would have been able to work with you before I stepped up to the plate at the largest and most prestigious sporting event in the world, but I can't change that now.

I am excited to report that when I prepare to hit now, I experience the confident and effortless feelings I once had as a child."--- Cindy Eadie

Cindy's experience of reconnecting epitomizes former major league manager Chuck Tanner's belief: *"You can't be afraid to fail. If you worry about failing, you will. The biggest reason behind these throwing mysteries is players trying not to make mistakes. You can't play that way.* **You have to play the way you did when you were a kid and not be afraid."**

CHAPTER EIGHTEEN

YOU DON'T HAVE TO LOSE
YOUR CURRENT POSITION

"We...are all trying to make sense out of nonsense, trying to put the world into some perspective, trying to form out of the chaos...some order and harmony."
--- Rollo May

Many players feel embarrassed when all of a sudden they literally forget how to throw a ball. Some fans and media judge them as if they were purposefully doing it. They don't understand at those particular moments the players are controlled by an invisible puppeteer.

Former Texas Rangers player Monty Fariss lost his position at shortstop. He no longer performed as the dominant player that made him the Rangers' 1988 first-round draft pick when he suddenly became hesitant to throw the ball to first base. Much to his dismay, the Rangers were forced to move him to second base where he once again played well.

I'M SO CONFIDENT RIGHT NOW THAT IT'S UNREAL

Chuck Shirley, a senior at Oklahoma Baptist University, emailed me January 29 as he was in a quandary, not only with his throwing, but with his hitting:

"I play at Oklahoma Baptist University. I play third, first, catch and DH. I've played mainly first and third the past two years ever since I got to OBU mainly because I feel like the coaching staff has a lack of confidence in my throwing ability.

I had Tommy John surgery when I was in high school and despite making one of the best and fastest recoveries I have never been the same throwing the ball. The injury was a freak occurrence; the doctors were never able to give me a reason for the injury as I had hardly ever pitched and tried to throw less than five curve balls in my entire life.

My dad pitched in the Major Leagues for 12 years so I have always had very good mechanics and release, as well as genetics. My arm strength was my most valuable asset on the field and most considered it to be my ticket. I missed pretty much my entire senior year because of rehab. But I managed to play in about 20 games; none behind the plate. All at either 1st or most DH.

Because of the injury and not playing my senior year, no schools wanted to touch me. I ended up at a Division II school in Kansas that ended up being a very good fit, but this is where the problems start.

At the beginning of my first semester it was only a year after surgery and I was still rehabbing. The coaches regarded me as a diamond in the rough and that I was one of their best signings ever, and that I would be one of the best players to ever have played there.

But when we started to play catch I couldn't throw the ball to a guy standing 20 feet away from me. I would let it go and the ball would hit five feet in front of him. So to compensate I would throw the ball over his head.

Then I would get real anxious and the ball started coming out of my hand wrong. It was like I was throwing sliders. I had a real loose grip and the ball would have slider spin to it. I started lobbing the ball until I felt like the guy was far enough away that If I threw it hard he would have time to react to it if it was a bad throw.

After four or five really hard throws I would relax a little and let up and from about 50 feet and out I was OK, not as accurate as I could be, but the ball didn't skip five feet in front of him. And if I threw it on a line it was more likely not to go over his head.

And then we started throwing bullpens, and I don't know whatever I did I couldn't throw the ball back to the pitchers. None of them would let me catch them. And if I did I had to lob it back to them with a high arch. I was so embarrassed. This thing that any 12-year-old kid could do I couldn't. This thing that I had done my entire life had disappeared.

I hated having to throw. Guys would steal and stop half between the base and dare me to throw it, and I couldn't do it. I transferred at semester more or less because I was embarrassed and it was hard for me to show my face around my teammates. I wondered what they thought of me and I had a lot of doubt about being around them.

When I transferred to Juco we would play catch in the gym in the winter, and we had to run every time some one missed a ball or made a bad throw and it hit the wall. I was petrified, but determined and hard-nosed so I played catch with the best fielder on the team. I told him what was up and he saved my butt a ton.

And I was beginning to push the ball. I lost velocity and started having problems with my arm soreness that I had never had before. But if I wouldn't have had to made those throws with something on the line, I would have ended up quitting to save myself the embarrassment.

I made it through Juco and I played a lot of third and first because that's where I was needed more, not really because of my inaccurate arm, but if I did catch I had the occasional over throw and short hop that made me a very hesitant player. Whereas before I just let it go knowing that it was gonna hit the guy in the chest.

I transferred to OBU and at first was told that I was needed more at third than behind the plate but then it became evident that I couldn't make routine throws. Just throwing it back to the pitcher was a chore. I never really know where it's gonna go. I made a lot of errors just throwing the ball. I would make great plays and end up not being able to finish, so I sat.

I have worked really hard this off-season to get back and now I've been moved to first because there are less throws across the field. It sucks. I'm frustrated with where I'm at and where I know I can be.

The mental stress has carried over to hitting. I know it as I used to just hammer the ball and attack pitches, but now I don't swing at pitches I should and pitchers can work me. My confidence is shot and I don't know what to do.

I have the talent and the desire to play major league baseball, but mentally I don't know anymore. Well, that's the bulk of the story. I'm open to pretty much anything right now. Sorry for being this long, but I feel like the more I tell you maybe the more you will be able to help."

We hooked up for an hour on the phone and utilized his imagination to help with his dilemma on February 6. We tackled such issues as Chuck's having zero control with light throws; overthrowing; something in the back of his mind fueling negative expectations; his release point problem of lightly gripping the ball and its falling out of his hand; and being judgmental and critical of himself. Chuck emailed me a week later:

"I don't know if you got last email or not, but everything is great just a few hiccups that I wanted to talk to you about. And if you can do to my swing what you've done to my throwing, I'll ride you all the way to the hall of fame!"

When I ask him what exactly happened, he said his other email he sent must not have gone through. So he paraphrased what he had said in it:

"My last email didn't say much.... just how the game has made an entire 180 on me and that I can't believe how much one conversation can make a difference!

I can't even begin to describe how I felt the first time I let the ball go from my hand and hit the guy right in the chest. And then again and again and again. It was so effortless. I was giddy just playing catch. I can't remember a time when I was happy to just be throwing the ball around.

Now I can't stop throwing. I take every opportunity to throw it and it goes where I want it every time. And if the ball doesn't go quite where I want it to go I can now feel it mechanically in my hand that I may have held it a little too long and or short and I adjust and make the next throw perfect. I used to wonder where the next one was going and when it didn't go where I intended it to go I had no idea why.

I'm so confident in throwing the ball right now it's unreal, like I said it's effortless. I don't even think about it and it goes. I can't thank you enough for your help and what you've done.

"Oh yeah. I wasn't kidding about the Hall of Fame either."

We worked for two additional 30 minute sessions addressing his hitting the ball for power, seeing the ball better, not reacting to the pitch and also his feeling disappointment from others. I heard back two weeks later:

"Well, I was waiting until we had a game to write to you and give you an update. The throwing is still amazing. We spent last week inside and out. We had games cancelled because of weather. But the time spent in the cage and Batting Practice was great.

I could totally tell the difference in the power. I mean I was really hitting the crap out of the ball and with tremendous frequency. I've been seeing the ball a lot better and longer during BP and hitting the ball the other way with ease because of it." --- Chuck Shirley

CHAPTER NINETEEN

WOHLERS FINDS THE
STRIKE ZONE

"Baseball is 90 percent mental and the other half is physical." --- Yogi Berra

John Schuerholz, general manager of the Atlanta Braves, summed up Atlanta Braves closer Mark Wohlers' problems that incapacitated him until he resurrected in May, 1999:

> *"It can't be physical, because in spring training he was as dominant as you can be. He does well on the side, he does great in the bullpen and he did fine in spring training. But when the game is on the line and the game is meaningful, he has an inability to feel where he ought to release the ball. Every time he sees a guy with a bat in his hand, it sort of brings those monsters home to roost. I feel bad for him because he's worked hard and he's a good guy."*

Mark Wohlers was one of the game's premier closers before becoming victim of the inexplicable like Blass and Ankiel. He recorded 98 saves from 1995-97 with his incredible 100 mph arm for the Atlanta Braves. Wohlers began struggling with his control late in 1997 and completely unraveled in 1998 at the age of 29.

Mark finished the 1998 season with 14.61 walks per nine innings. He spent most of the year alternating between the Braves major and minor leagues. While at Class AAA Richmond he walked 36 in 12 1/3 innings.

Initially there was hope for Wohlers the following spring of 1999 as he appeared to have conquered his demons. However, once the season began, optimism for Wohlers maintaining his mechanics faded quickly. The Braves traded him to the Cincinnati Reds on April 16 after Wohlers refused to accept another assignment to the minors.

On May 6, 1999, *USA Today's* Chuck Johnson ran a feature story on Wohlers entitled: "Yikes, it's the Yips! Aimless hurlers struggle to put finger on the cause." Suddenly a big-league pitcher can't throw strikes:

> *"There were signs of initial progress, but Wohlers suffered a setback Sunday [May 2] in his first game action since the trade. He pitched one-third of an inning for Class AAA Indianapolis against Toledo (Ohio) and threw 22 balls in 31 pitches, giving up four runs on five walks, a hit and four wild pitches. For the time being, he'll stay with the Reds to continue working with pitching coach Don Gullett."*

The last part of that article went as follows:

> *"Crowley says he would like a crack at helping Wohlers. He was able to contact the Reds on the recommendation of Blass. "Their team doctor called April 17 to ask if I would be available and I told them I would be," he says.*
>
> *In recent years, more and more teams and athletes have turned to psychologists to solve problems that go beyond the physical. But some baseball people remain skeptical.*
>
> *"Every guy in the country is now coming out of the woodwork saying 'I can fix him,'" Reds' manager Jack McKeon says. "My belief is the only guy who can fix him is the guy who's out there pitching."*
>
> *Still, Crowley is convinced Wohlers' career is salvageable. "If Steve Blass is cured, and he's the poster child for all this stuff, that means that anyone in the field of sports can be cured," he says.*

When interviewed for this article, I purposefully answered as if I were speaking directly to Wohlers. It obviously worked. Wohlers told me when he read it that he brought it to the attention of his organization. The Reds flew me in the following day, May 7, to start working with him.

On May 12, just six days after this feature article appeared, *USA Today* reported again on Wohlers' throwing. This time it was a different story. Wohlers had made an about face:

"Mark Wohlers might have found the cure to his inability to throw strikes. After a session with Richard Crowley, Wohlers threw on the side Tuesday and had his most impressive showing since his April 16 trade from Atlanta. Crowley, who helped former Los Angeles Dodgers second baseman Steve Sax work through a problem throwing to first base in 1983, was recommended to the Reds by former major league pitcher Steve Blass, who went through a similar control problem as Wohlers' in 1973."

That same day in the *Dayton Daily News*, Hal McCoy, a member of the writers wing of the Major League Baseball Hall of Fame, wrote his version of Wohlers' re-emerging control:

"Richard Crowley is working with the control-plagued pitcher and well. Tuesday was a beautiful day in the neighborhood for Wohlers -- and there haven't been any of those since the Cincinnati Reds acquired him from Atlanta on April 16.

Wohlers, on the disabled list with anxiety disorders (he can't throw the ball over home plate), stunned pitching coach Don Gullett during a 12-minute bullpen session Tuesday and was the best he has been.

"What Wohlers did today was the best he's done ... unbelievably good," Gullett said. "He didn't throw one ball bad, not one."

Wohlers pitched to Pitcher's Pal, the inflated crash-test dummy he maimed the last time he threw, "and he threw inside on the dummy, which is what we wanted to see, and didn't hit it. That's what we've been looking for--control on inside pitches to right-handers," Gullett said.

Wohlers was excited after the session and when manager Jack McKeon saw him perspiring heavily in the clubhouse after the workout, McKeon asked how it went and Wohlers said, "Great. I want to go right back out there right now."

Wohlers went on to successfully pitch to live hitters. However, the wear and tear on his arm from the past year and a half throwing out of sync caught up with him. He underwent Tommy John surgery and finished the last two years of his career playing for the Cincinnati Reds and New York Yankees in 2001 and the Cleveland Indians in 2002.

However, the inexplicable always leaves players wondering why, always trying to understand how it happened in the first place. Wohlers commented, *"I convinced myself the reason I couldn't pitch straight was because I blew out my elbow, even though deep down I don't know what it was."* Wohlers concluded, *"The mind is a powerful thing."*

In 2001 Wohlers amassed four wins, one loss, an ERA of 4.26 and a walk ratio of 3.32 per nine innings. In 2002 he finished with 3-4 record, an ERA of 4.79 and a walk ratio of 3.28. During his best year, 1995, his walk ratio was 3.34.

Wohlers left baseball for what he deemed personal reasons at the start of the 2003 season.

ANATOMY
OF
THE
DISCONNECT

"Mr. Duffy lived a short distance from his body." --- James Joyce

CHAPTER TWENTY

POINT OF ENTRY OF THE DISCONNECT

"No matter what area of your life seems to you to be blocked or thwarted, stop and reconsider: you will recognize the outer 'enemy' as but a reflection of what you have not, before now, been willing or able to recognize as coming from within." --- Ralph Blum

When the invisible *reality* -- your invisible opponent -- crosses over and manifests into the visible *reality* -- your game -- that is its point of entry initiating your struggles. It is the point of entry of this adversary or opposing force that can separate you from your self-esteem and mechanics. It then forms a new reality.

What immediately follows is "a disconnect." The player is bewildered, and thinks "What's that all about?" Confused, he returns to his game.

Then either immediately, or many games down the road, it bubbles back to surface from its invisible landscape.

And there "it" is again. But what is "it"? You may shrug "it" off, but on some level you are well aware that something disturbing has entered your psyche, some uninvited guest has entered your house. And it does not feel good at all.

Negative thoughts, streaky performances and head-scratching mechanics are clues that a parallel reality is occurring. It is equivalent to two motion pictures playing simultaneously.

I KNEW SOMETHING HAD SHIFTED

Nate Milone mysteriously found himself disconnected from his impeccable mechanics and suffered the loss of a promising career as a pro ball player:

"From 1984 to 1988 I was at my prime as a catcher in the Los Angeles area. In 1986 I was honored with All-League and given a spot in the 1986 All-Star game sponsored by the Daily News, a newspaper here in the San Fernando Valley.

I had a number of scouts and colleges interested in me. In 1986 I chose to attend College of the Canyons, a local college in Valencia, California. At the time I was the only starting freshman on the team. Things were going very well.

Then during mid-season in a game against USC something strange happened. In the middle of the seventh inning I was not able to throw the ball back to the pitcher. I lost all control and feeling of throwing the ball. It was as if I were a four-year-old throwing a ball for the first time ever! The strange thing about it was that I was able to throw the ball well in practice and to all the bases well.

My coach said he had experienced this situation before and was aware that a sports psychologist had successfully resolved a similar problem with Steve Sax, the Dodgers second baseman at the time. He said that he was going to locate this doctor and make an appointment for me. The doctor's name was Richard Crowley. Unfortunately, he was never able to be located.

As time went on my confidence deteriorated. My love of the game was lost. And I fell from the sport of baseball.

· Eight years past, and by some freak coincidence I was telling my story to a friend, Sean Crowley, I recently met who just moved from Indiana to California. After telling him my story, it was shocking to learn that Dr.

Crowley was his uncle! Finally, after eight years I was able to locate and meet him.

After spending some time with Dr. Crowley and telling him what had happened he said, "I can fix that."

I only spent 10 minutes at the most going through some technique that he had developed. At the end of his using his approach I knew something had shifted.

I was still skeptical, but eager to play and see what the results would be. With his help I was cured of whatever was wrong from eight years ago and I now lead my adult league in all categories, i.e. batting, throwing percentages, etc.

Life could have been different if I had 10 minutes of his time eight years ago."
--- Nate Milone

Athletes eventually become well-versed with their mechanics. So the mechanics, by themselves, are not necessarily the problem. The problem is: How do excellent mechanics transmute into struggles and slumps? The answer is found by targeting the invisible opponent's point of entry, and not the athletes' mechanics.

EVERYBODY STRUGGLES FROM TIME TO TIME

Los Angeles Angels pitcher Brendan Donnelly was struggling with his invisible opponent during the 2005 season when his ERA had soared from 2.45 to 4.07. He ended the season with a 3.72 ERA compared to 3.00, 1.58, 2.17, respectively for years 2004, 2003 and 2002.

Donnelly didn't know what to make of it either. He was fuming and perplexed over it when he said, *"I don't have a theory. I don't have an answer. You ever know a hitter to be in a slump? I'm in a slump. If I had an answer, I'd give it to you."*

When a pitcher gets a splinter in the finger of his pitching hand, the sooner he removes it, the sooner the healing process begins.

Metaphorically speaking, if a splinter enters a healthy ball player's psyche and separates him from his highly functioning mechanics, you would also remove the splinter at its exact point of entry and his natural mechanics would be fully reconnected once again. Stop looking for a logical cause simply because it's familiar and the light is better.

Remember ever having a splinter? Did you choose to get that annoying splinter? No. Was it your intention to have that annoying splinter? No. So you really can't say "I'm responsible for giving myself that splinter." Of course not. Therefore, you are not responsible for the disconnect either. Bottom line, it is unintentional.

I THREW ABSOLUTELY UNBELIEVABLY

For some players, an injury becomes the point of entry for the splinter that disconnects them from their mechanics. Long after the injury has healed, some players continue to struggle.

Mario Gardea, a 24-year-old, 230 pound right-hand pitcher, periodically "forgot" how to pitch following an injury to his shoulder. His story parallels Mackey Sasser, Shawn Green and far too many other players following an injury:

"I have a problem every time I have a good pitching session. Afterward I start to try to "remember" how I did it. I have had this problem ever since I hurt my shoulder in high school, and after that I have never been able to get consistent in my physical game or mental game.

I played in the Yankees organization from 1999-2000 then with Cincinnati from 2000-2001. I always "felt" I was better that the so-called prospects. I was told when I was 19 by pitching coaches in the Yankees' organization that I have major league caliber pitches and that I would be on my way to the majors very soon.

Only problem was that for the first two weeks of spring training I was absolutely unhittable. Then one morning I woke up and started to lose my control and as the days went by it got worse until I felt lost up there.

I would like to work on it by being on the top of my game when I do pitch. It feels like a splinter in my brain that I feel will not go away. It gets embedded deeper and deeper every time I feel good about the way I pitch. The next thing that pops in my head is, "Remember how you threw; remember how you threw."

Then the next time I go to throw I don't feel comfortable, so I change my arm angle, maybe a high leg kick, even throw knuckle balls so I can get that feeling back of being "on."

Mario emailed me after we had worked for an hour over the phone:

"Dr. Crowley, where do I start? Man, I threw absolutely unbelievably after our session. I threw amazingly well. I was placing my fastball where I wanted and my breaking stuff was great.

The thing that I noticed the most about the session was when I did not throw a good pitch I did not feel this tight feeling in my chest. I just went to the next pitch and delivered.

Ever since we spoke I feel a lot more confident and stronger. I don't know where the stronger part came in, but it's working. Thanks for your help."
--- Mario Gardea

CHAPTER TWENTY-ONE

NO ONE IS IMMUNE FROM
THE DISCONNECT

"Healing does not come from increasing the amount of light in our lives, but rather from reaching into the shadow and drawing up unreconciled elements of ourselves into the light where they can be healed." --- Tao-te-Ching

As we begin to grow and experience life, pebbles of disappointment and stones of worry and fear begin to fill our lives. As this happens we lose more and more of our energy -- the source of our spirit. We become more and more removed from the here-and-now, the present moment.

Sometimes we may not even be aware of the disconnection from this particular part of our spirit. Other times we are well aware of an emptiness and separation by the loss of our vitality and talents.

Once we become aware of what has happened, we can then start removing these shadow impediments from our thinking by transforming them into the original gifts of our spirit.

Our natural abilities and energy can return.

During August 2004, the following article, "The Furthest Thing from Sports Psychology," appeared in a three-part interview by Brian Walton, managing editor of the prestigious online website, thestlcardinals.com:

Brian Walton: Earlier, Dr. Crowley, you mentioned the word "disconnected" and I also saw it referenced on your website. How do you determine disconnection? How does this happen?

Dr. Crowley: Think of electrical wiring and what can happen if the wire gets loose a little bit....it's that same kind of feeling. So then, for example, the radio or TV doesn't work properly.

Then you realize, "Oh, it's a loose wire. I don't even know how it got loose." There is nothing wrong with the radio or TV. There is nothing wrong with the player. The problem is in the disconnection.

It's whatever jarred it loose that disconnected it; disconnected the player. Many would call it self-doubt and thinking too much was what jars it loose. I don't believe that's the case. The disconnect that separates a player from his natural mechanics comes before self-doubt and thinking too much entered his consciousness.

A classic example would be Derek Jeter who was in a slump early in the 2004 season. Someone who is in such a prolonged slump is beside himself. He's not himself. He's off. He's disconnected. And it shows up watching him hit, or rather, not hit. Something has somehow splintered him and separated him in some strange way from his mechanics.

Jeter described it: "After you find yourself in that negative zone, you're going 'What's this all about?'"

Maybe at the beginning some players may not know they're in that negative zone. They still feel they are doing OK. They only become aware of it because their numbers started reflecting it. Other players are aware of its presence immediately as it is a foreign feeling at the plate. They are aware of the disconnect from the absence of that feel, yet they can't understand it nor find words to express it.

Brian Walton: When you get reconnected, is it like a light switch that is turned on immediately?

Dr. Crowley: It's as simple as putting the plug back in. It's like someone trips over the cord, and everyone is trying to fix the TV or radio -- the mechanics -- and no one has noticed that somehow the cord has accidentally become disconnected. The disconnect can happen that quickly with athletes.

A player's disconnect is not logical. It makes no sense to go from hot to cold. That is why all my work takes place in what has been called the illogical or irrational part of a player's mind.

I address their specific disconnect just like any coach would, but with a different approach, that of being a mental mechanics coach. I address their mechanical issues they present along with what I call their fallout....which would be the secondary issues of self-doubt, worrying, negative thinking and lack of confidence.

Reconnecting the disconnect is the fastest way of getting a player back on track. Other methods of coaching may work as well. Yet, if a player or an organization wants to expedite ending a slump at the plate or on the mound, then the method I have developed seems to realize that outcome sooner.

I DON'T HAVE TO BE PERFECT

The disconnect can happen to any player, at any level. When Chad Hermansen was with the Dodgers in 2003, he contacted me to deal with a throwing problem. It was believed to be mechanical, but it never could respond to coaches instructions nor his hard work to resolve it. We worked together and Chad summarized what happened:

"My name is Chad Hermansen and I play for the Dodgers. I have almost two years big league experience and I am currently in a triple-A in Las Vegas were I actually live. I have had throwing problem for what seems like forever as I was drafted as a shortstop by the Pittsburgh Pirates in 1995. I made a ton of errors at short mostly throwing and was moved from short to the outfield to second

and back to the outfield. I have now been in the outfield since 1998 and I have always felt more comfortable out there.

I have always been the type of player that has had a very good arm but didn't know where it was going half the time and to this day I don't feel comfortable throwing. This last off-season I had surgery on my shoulder with a labrum tear. I have come back pretty strong, but am still working on my flexibility and arm strength. I definitely need some help that has been long overdue.

Some of my problems throwing have been when I go into my motion to throw, my throwing hand will go to my ear and then it seems as if I just push the ball. I have been told to get the hand away from my head and I try that and I seem to fall back and never find the same release point. I have always thought that my mechanics were bad and I just haven't been able to fix them. I know a lot of it is in the head, but I have searched for answers and haven't found any.

I contacted Dr. Crowley immediately and we began to work on the telephone several times before we met in person as I was on the road. I had bad mechanics that had plagued me and didn't respond to everything I had tried over the years. All the coaches I worked with couldn't get my throwing back to where it had been in the past.

Because of my ongoing problem whenever I played short, I would throw side-armed. And as an outfielder I felt limited to only chucking it. I never felt a 100% comfortable. I had been pushing it out at a different arm angle each time, a different release point each time. I never had a good follow-through. In fielding I wouldn't be able to pick my target. It would one-hop when I tried to throw it on line.

However, beginning August 19, Dr. Crowley and I discussed all these problems. He mentally coached me through my mechanics with his technique. He helped me from the very beginning. August 21st, only two days after our first telephone session, I played one game and fielded three balls. Two out of the three were real good....right on line. I hadn't done that all year!

On August 23, we worked on my over-thinking and the weird position my arm takes when I throw. My arm would go right to my ear and then I would end up pushing it from there. I became aware how my entire right arm felt incredibly tight. This chronic awkwardness in my mechanics may have resulted in my previous shoulder surgery. A friend told me that he couldn't look at me throw like I did as it was painful for him to watch!

I found myself taking a step forward. I felt positive. When I would throw a bad one, the old me would have said, "Here we go again." But now I was no longer getting frustrated. I would simply make an adjustment and tell myself, "I don't have to be perfect."

Four days later (August 27), I felt loose and comfortable. The ball went to where I wanted the night before during a game. I became more confident with each throw. It was a powerful feeling. The previous night was probably my best game of the year. Baseball was becoming more fun!

I told Dr. Crowley about other problems I was having with lack of good extension and interrupted focus with my target. I would lose my target by the time I threw the ball...then I saw it...then I didn't ...then I saw it again. It was the strangest thing to me, but not to Dr. Crowley who enthusiastically dove into the problem with me with a very confident attitude.

Three days later I was home from the road games and Dr. Crowley drove to Las Vegas to work with me. On August 30, my strength coach Jason Romano of the Los Angeles Dodgers at the time, Dr. Crowley and I drove to an isolated, small park where he observed Jason and me playing catch. After ten minutes into throwing with Jason, I showed Dr. Crowley the problem that I still couldn't overcome: I would either release the ball too late or hold to it too long. This had been a chronic, core problem badgering me back to the days when I played with the Pirates where nobody was able to help me resolve it.

Dr. Crowley told Jason and me to take a break and sit down on the grass beside him. He then walked me through his imagination process to try to end my awkward throwing. We focused on my release problem. It took about five minutes.

He told us to go back throwing again to see what the result would be. Upon my first throw Jason congratulated me. And then Jason enthusiastically did so a second and third time! I looked at Dr. Crowley and said, "My arm is back to its original mechanics. I haven't felt this in years!" Jason jumped in saying, "That's the best I've seen!"

The next time I spoke with Dr. Crowley on the telephone was September 1st. He asked me how I was doing. My comment was, "Awesome. I feel reconnected!" Two nights before I had played in a game and told him, "I had a couple of balls come to me to throw. It felt awesome. I thought of nothing else. I visualized my arm as my target. I just threw!" --- Chad Hermansen

CHAPTER TWENTY-TWO

THE DISCONNECT OF PLAYERS' ARMS

"Man is his own doctor and finds proper healing herbs in his own garden; the physician is in ourselves, and in our own nature are all things that we need."
--- Paracelsus

The invisible opponent's point of entry created a disconnect for two major league ball players: former Anaheim Angels Ken Tatum and Baltimore Orioles Paul Blair. Tatum was the best reliever in the American League in 1969 for the Angels. His reign continued into the following year when he hit Paul Blair in the jaw.

Blair was never the same hitter, but Tatum could never again pitch inside. *"Whenever I tried,"* Tatum reflected, *"I couldn't get my arm to do it."*

THOUGHTS OF 'WHAT IF IT HAPPENS AGAIN?' WERE GONE

Lauren Suedkamp personally identified with Paul Blair's experience. Lauren's jaw was struck by a ball while at bat and it affected her pitching:

"While a freshman playing varsity fastball softball at Providence High School in Burbank, I was hit in the face at bat. Even though I wore a protective mask, it was later found that I got a hairline fracture of my jaw.

Prior to the injury I had a 1.14 ERA and a batting average of .222. After being hit I could not seem to pitch after the first inning. I couldn't throw strikes any longer and I had always been a most accurate pitcher. I had no real clue what was wrong. It no longer felt like my arm was there. I immediately knew from the release point that the ball wasn't going where I wanted it to go.

My parents got me an appointment with Dr. Crowley. After the first of just two meetings, the persisting thoughts of "What if it happens again?" were gone and the "numbness" in my hand felt gone as well. I pitched with my coach a few hours after our initial meeting and I was pitching practically back to where I was originally. It was much easier. It felt even effortless. The feeling of being susceptible was gone.

The very next day I met with Dr. Crowley again and we worked on other issues that had affected my confidence and fun pitching. The next day in a game I pitched five innings, was 2-for-3, and got three RBI. We won 12-to-9. Our last game of the season was three days later. Even though we lost 9-to-7, I felt like my pitching was perfect."

A few weeks later Lauren sent me an update that showed how the work we did crossed over to enhance her batting average:

"My team made it to the first round of playoffs and lost. But I had the second highest batting average in my league and I had the most RBI. My coach chose to play me in left field rather than pitch because she felt it would be better for the team this year." --- Lauren Suedkamp

Kevin "Hot Sauce" Saucier was traded from the Philadelphia Phillies to the Detroit Tigers during the 1981 season. As the Tigers' closer Saucier posted a 1.65 ERA in 49 innings, surrendering only one home run in 1981.

In the middle of 1982, Saucier was still pitching well with a 3.12 ERA in 40 innings with no home runs given up. Suddenly, he started to worry about wildness. Saucier said, *"I'm afraid I'm going to kill somebody out there."* He had no idea where his pitches were going. He developed an extreme fear of hitting a batter. His invisible opponent was on the mound with him controlling his arm.

Saucier lost his control and retired in mid-season with no minor league rehab assignment nor time on the DL. His invisible opponent stole the dream he had since childhood. No one knew what to do to help him regain his control.

THE MORE I THREW THE MORE CONFIDENT I BECAME

Matt Johnson's inner trickster had him up against a wall. It taunted him when it came time to pitch making him anxious of hitting a batter also:

"I am a former Division II college player, now teaching and coaching a high school baseball team. For about a year now, I have been unable to pitch batting practice.

Outside the cage, I can hit spots, but from behind the L-screen, I look like a buffoon. Obviously my professional career does not depend on this, but I look at the other coaches (who have been surprisingly supportive) and feel like a jerk because they have to pitch to more batters than they should. Can you help me?"

We worked together using his imagination for half an hour over the phone. We focused on two issues: Matt's release point and his loss of control whenever facing a batter. Within a few hours Matt emailed me the following:

I just wanted to give you an update on my progress.... After I spoke to you, we had optional hitting practice. After everyone had hit, I asked if anyone was brave enough to get in the cage with me (that was the hardest part....getting someone to put themselves in the line of fire).

One volunteer agreed and I threw about 150-200 pitches to him. I did not hit him at all. It was strange. It was just different than it had been. The more I

threw, the more confident I became and the better I pitched. Thanks so much."
---- Matt Johnson

Players who struggle like Tatum, Blair, Suedkamp and Johnson are very aware of this weird phenomenon of their brain not responding to their desires.

IMPROVEMENT WAS NOTICED BY MY TEAMMATES

"It's as if a different brain is running me," said Marc Mullins, an amateur catcher in the men's senior leagues with whom I had the opportunity to work. Marc emailed me the following issues:

"I'm 51-years-old and have played amateur ball every year since age eight. I play senior baseball for a team out of Puget Sound Region. We are a top nationally ranked team in 48 plus age group. Problem started at age 18 while playing high school ball. Playing in Texas in front of a lot of pro scouts (to see the starting pitchers) and all of a sudden I couldn't throw the ball back to the pitcher with men on base.

I had a labrum surgery last year. Shoulder is all fixed now but my brain is really screwed up and the throwing problem is worse. Now I have what I guess is a fear of failure.

When I get ready to throw back to the pitcher the ball feels awkward in my hand. I tend to shotput or push the ball rather than let the ball roll off my fingers. My arm is very stiff and not a nice fluid motion as when I am throwing well. The worse it gets the more I lob the ball in up to a twenty foot arc.

My thought when I throw poorly is that my arm is not connected to my brain. It won't perform as I am willing it too. I can't find the release point, the right arm angle, etc. My whole throwing motion is stiff and awkward. My foot work is poor. I don't step at the target and often times don't align my shoulder parallel with the target before throw. My teammates point to my bad mechanics as being the cause. Not the case."

Mark and entered his imagination and he was directed to allow his imagination, and not his intellect, spontaneously present him with symbolic images representing his numerous conflicts. A week later Marc emailed me his results:

"I have caught two ball games since I worked with you and DH'd in another. Results of our session are promising. I feel comfortable and loose warming up and am much better warming up pitchers in a confined bullpen and in between innings. Confined bullpens with fences on the side were quite problematic in the past for some reason.

I still want to soft toss the ball with men on base, but since our session it is no longer the out-of-control, stiff, spasmodic throw as before. I let 'er rip back to the pitcher with no one on base or when we have a good lead. That's an improvement. The improvement is noticed by my teammates." --- Marc Mullins

Your invisible opponent comes and goes as it chooses. It is a master manipulator. When it is there, it can beat you up and turn you against yourself.

CAN'T CONTROL MY ARM

During the 2005 season, the Los Angeles Angels of Anaheim were 51-2 when leading after eight innings. But for some reason in one isolated instance, Francisco Rodriguez couldn't locate the strike zone. It occurred in the ninth inning when he walked four batters that included a four-pitch walk to Alex Rodriguez that forced in the first run of the inning.

"It was a disaster," said K-Rod, who suffered his fourth blown save. *"I didn't make any pitchers at all. I feel I beat myself. I don't think they beat me."*

"It's frustrating when you don't do your job."

"It's worse when you feel you can't throw strikes, can't control your body, can't control your arm."

K-Rod's invisible opponent had done its job. It not only had him unable to control the ball, but it talked him into beating himself up. Most players' struggles, such as K-Rod's, are a way to observe the invisible opponent phenomena in action.

FELT LIKE SOME OTHER PERSON WOULD GRAB MY ARM

Ryan Heil, a young pitcher with the Mets rookie league team, describes how his invisible opponent had a mind of its own in opposition to his intention. It controlled his arm:

"The "creature" for me mostly showed up whenever I took the mound in practice settings as well as in competition. The feeling I had was very strange and I have always felt like it has been more physical than mental."

Remember, even though it may manifest as "physic-al" or "ment-al," it is being generated from the "imagin-al," housed in your imagination.

"With the exception of the embarrassment and fear that steadily grew in my stomach, my delivery started just as it always had. I would lift my leg, start home and my arm would begin to go around. But just as my arm reached somewhere around my ear, right before the release point, my hand would grab the ball sending it roughly ten feet left of the catcher.

I would try to throw the ball over and over, but my hand would continue to grab the ball and take it left. When I would try to leave my hand completely out of the equation, my hand would not grab the ball, but it would send it about five feet right of the catcher and well over the batter's head, much like the replays of Ankiel's pitches in the playoffs.

I felt like some other person would grab my arm, from the forearm down, and redirect the entire appendage. After a few days the anxiety grew and soon ate me up from the inside out. It made my summer very unenjoyable, and baseball quite arduous, which it has never been."

I worked with Ryan for an hour and a half initially and then followed-up a few weeks later. Both our meetings were in person. He emailed me from spring training:

"I have been throwing well for quite some time now. In fact, I can't remember a time that I have thrown better.

I have a partner that will toss with me almost every day and I am getting very confident. I can't wait for the season. I think I will have a year like I have never had.

If there is a word of advice that I could give other players, it is to have faith. They will get through whatever is going on since there is now a solution.

As for my command down here in spring training, it's great. A coach came up to me yesterday and told me, "Ryan, if I had not seen what happened to you last summer, you would never know by watching you," which is good.

You are a miracle worker. Thank you for opening the door to getting my talent back." --- Ryan Heil

CHAPTER TWENTY-THREE

THE DISCONNECT BEHIND
THE PLATE

"Beneath every conflict is a desire to connect." ---Dannan Perry

Former New York Yankees catcher Fran Healy reflected on his struggles: *"The problem, to a degree, existed throughout my career. But I was able to hide it. I'd just flip it back real easy to the pitchers. I'd walk out after every pitch and say something to the pitcher, like 'Stay low' or 'Keep on it' or Bad call.' As a catcher you can disguise a problem like this. Pitchers can't. Their careers are over."*

Many catchers can't hide it as well as Fran Healy had over nine seasons during the '70's when he caught 415 games. Former Atlanta Braves Dale Murphy, a seven-time All-Star, wasn't so lucky. He began his professional career as a catcher and was moved to a different position. Murphy was sent to the outfield because he became disconnected from his natural ability to throw the ball back to the pitcher.

NO LONGER PHASED BY BAD THROWS

Mike Santoro, an 18-year-old catcher from New Jersey, was in the throws of the catcher's malady:

"I am writing to you because in the last eight games of my high school season I have had a persistent problem simply throwing the ball back to the pitcher.

I throw the ball over his head, in the dirt, high, low, to the left, and to the right. I have had my pitchers stay after practice with me so that I can practice throwing back to them. I have tried "clearing the mechanism" trying to zone everything out. I've tried concentrating on my mechanics and not concentrating on my mechanics, but resultantly, every four or five, and sometimes two or three throws, I mess up.

When it happens once, I start thinking about it. I tell myself to stop thinking about it and play the game. But I continue to think about it even more. I can't concentrate on the more important aspects of my catching because I'm always only thinking about my throws. It absorbs my mentality and its very frustrating.

I play very, very tentative lately, and it scares the hell out of me that I can't do something that I have been doing for years, thousands upon thousands of times. My throwing to the bases tends to only suffer when I have an extremely bad game throwing back to the pitcher.

Out of the eight bad games maybe two were beyond embarrassing. Although generally, my throws to bases are perfect even when I don't throw back to the pitcher well.

I feel like the catcher from that movie "Major League II" and I can't understand why.

I am a Division One catcher. I am the hardest worker I know. Baseball is solely without question my entire life. Please help me rid myself of this painful problem. I want to have fun again. I want to stop embarrassing myself and affecting all other aspects of my game for such a stupid problem. I could really use some guidance. No one else seems to know what to do."

As a result of working a couple of hours during a two week period, Mike noticed a significant shift in his catching:

"The game on Sunday went very well; no bad throws and I felt very confident. We also had a game on Tuesday night. During the entire game I was great until the fifth inning when I threw about three to four bad throws, one with a man on second who advanced to third.

I'm sure that the flaw is no longer mental because the bad throws didn't phase me like they would in the past. I feel much better now than I have in months.

During the last two-three games I have had no throwing problems at all. I'm doing well. And the work we did has improved other parts of my game as I just went 3-for-3 and had three RBI!

Maybe someday you can help another catcher with my problem." --- Mike Santoro

I GOT MY GAME BACK

Another catcher, Ryan Baukol, soon showed up at my door. His problems mirrored Michael's and provided encouragement for achieving similar results:

"I am a catcher at the College of San Mateo which is a JC in Northern California. I was reading the players' stories on your site when I came across the one written by Mike Santoro. When I read his story, I honestly felt that I was reading exactly what I would have written about my problem.

I can't even begin to describe how similar my situation is to his. I thought that his story could have been mine. I read the wonderful things you did for him and others, and I hope that the same can be done for me."

We worked on Ryan's problems that were parallel to Michael's. His feedback arrived in an email following our first session on the telephone:

125

"I have to tell you that I have felt much more comfortable throwing this week. I feel at ease when I'm throwing which is a feeling that I haven't had for a while.

On Monday I caught a few bullpens and I had no issues throwing the ball back to the pitcher. Even though it wasn't a game situation I found that to be very encouraging.

However, I played in a game today and I had no issues throwing the ball back to the pitcher. It was like I felt normal again."

Ryan wrapped up his total experience in his final email:

"I've now had a very strong November and December. I really felt that I got my game back and I'm playing with a lot more confidence."--- Ryan Baukol

CHAPTER TWENTY-FOUR

THE DISCONNECT AT
THE PLATE

"Study the swing from the ground up, rather than base your evaluations on results. It's cause and effect. If you coach the effect, you are chasing rainbows."
--- Former Major League slugger, Reggie Smith

Remember, your negative and critical thoughts are not the cause of your struggles as it is widely believed. They are the effect. The place to target is the cause itself, the disconnect that is orchestrated by your invisible opponent.

Sometimes you can see the invisible opponent tormenting a player for a few innings or maybe the entire game. Other times it spills over into several games or even into slumps, sometimes painfully prolonged ones.

Former Kansas City Royals' third baseman and member of the Hall of Fame George Brett coined the phrase "Mendoza line" to describe when a batter's average was below that of former Texas Rangers' shortstop Mario Mendoza's.

Mendoza was considered a good-fielding shortstop, but he hit below .200 three straight seasons (1975-77) totaling five times in his nine-year career. The unofficial "Mendoza Line" of .200, is often used as a barometer for the truly offensively challenged.

THE BEST SEASON OF MY LIFE

Jonathan Chiusano is a high school freshman and first baseman from Santa Clarita, California. He had dropped far below the unofficial Mendoza Line and was hitting .125 when his father contacted me:

"My son is 14-years-old and has played little league baseball since he was about eight-years-old. He has been taking hitting instruction for three years with some major league pros and they say to us that he has all the mechanics and eye-hand coordination and power to hit. Only problem is, in the game, he just can't seem to hit.

Towards the end of last season his hitting problems started. At the end of last season he was chosen to play on a travel ball team and only batted .125 for the season. To make it worse on him, the coach recently has brought some new players to the team and he was not selected to play in the next tournament this weekend.

We know he has it; his hitting coach knows he has it. Now it's time for us to help him know that he can do it. I would be interested in setting up a consultation with Jonathan." --- Anthony Chiusano

"On January 26th my parents brought me to meet with Dr. Crowley at his office in Burbank. I let him know that I did fine in practice, but I would somehow get tense during a game. He assured me that my batting problem would soon be a thing of the past.

During the hour session Dr. Crowley had me use his imagination technique and we worked on a number of things like tightening up at bat, overthinking and the pressure associated with all of that.

Two days later I emailed Dr. Crowley the following:

To start off with, I just got back from a game and things went great. To tell you the truth, I haven't felt that calm at the plate for awhile (or ever).

I remembered your techniques when I was at bat and I hit the ball. But the thing that shocked me the most was when I struck out, I had absolutely no failure feelings inside of me. I walked away and remembered some of the "pictures" and said to myself, 'I'll get him next time.' I am glad that I have learned a way to be relieved of my feelings of failure and pessimism.

I practiced another week and emailed Dr. Crowley what happened:

I had my first league game two nights ago. Overall, it was a fantastic game on my part. I went one-for-two with a walk: it was a fly out (no mental error just early on the ball) and a hard line drive single to right field.

Each time I came to the plate I had confidence. I imagined the pictures I created and everything turned out great.

I emailed Dr. Crowley again two months later to let him know how the rest of the season went:

First off I'll tell you that I have been having the best season of my life. I'm batting third, fourth, or fifth. I've been having fantastic games lately. I've had games where I went two for two with two doubles.

But the main reason I am contacting you is because of my last game. We were playing my friend's team, Robbie Mousselli. Robbie is the hardest throwing kid at Hart. He throws low 80's, which is pretty fast at my age. Well, my first at-bat I walked; second at-bat I got a single; then everyone got nervous because Robbie started pitching.

I got up to bat against Robbie. My coach had me bunt. Nothing exciting, but it was a good bunt. Anyways, my team was losing three to two. It was the bottom of the 7th (we only play seven innings.) And the very top of the line up was up. I was in the hole. One kid hits a double, another kid gets a walk. So there's a man on second and third. I am up.

But before I got up, I sat in the dugout just really concentrating on all of your methods. I calmed myself because I was a little nervous against Robbie. Then I get up to bat and they call time out.

The whole time they are talking, I am preparing myself. Time out is over and I am up to bat. Robbie sets and I concentrate, the pitch, it was thrown hard and inside.

I see the ball as if it was in slow motion; the ball looked like a bean bag. And I cranked the ball over all of the outfielder's heads (we were playing on a college sized baseball field). I won the game with my shot, scoring both of the runners on base. We won 4-to-3 because of my hit. I hit a ball over 310 ft against the hardest throwing 13-year-old in the valley. My team was all over me and we were ecstatic. I had so much fun.

Later I talked to Robbie. He said I hit the farthest ball off of him ever! THANK YOU." --- Jonathan Chiusano

CHAPTER TWENTY-FIVE

THE DISCONNECT ON
THE MOUND

"In dealing with fear, the only way out is in." --- Sheldon Kopp

Fear and anxiety, as well as confidence and relaxation, are orchestrated by another profound consciousness that is operating continuously in your imagination. It is one which you are not necessarily aware of existing, yet it has the innate potential to enhance or subterfuge your mechanics as well as your physical and personal well-being. However, you can focus your attention on it and have its energy work on your behalf rather than against you.

I PLAYED LIKE I DIDN'T HAVE A CARE IN THE WORLD

Ernie Herring, a freshman pitcher at St. Mary's College in Maryland, was up against a wall battling his demons. Ernie, like a number of players, mysteriously forgot how to throw the ball. We worked for an hour and a half and Ernie emailed a summary of his problem and what events took place that summer:

"I have been playing baseball for the past eight years of my life I have the makings of being able to pitch in the majors. I'm a 6'4", 200 pound lefty who throws in the low 80's. With a little work I could touch 90.

However, during my freshman year at college, I "forgot" how to throw a baseball! I had gotten so bad that I couldn't play a game of catch with our second baseman without worrying about throwing the ball to him on a line instead of lobbing it.

I was all over the place....low, high, kinda like how Sax and Wohlers were. I would get nervous, thinking too much, and BOOM! The pitch sailed off the back stop or in the dirt. I lost all the confidence I had built up and all my dreams were hanging in the balance.

I searched and searched on ways to help myself and my throwing. I came across the good doctor's web site. I took a chance and emailed him. The day after we worked on my throwing problem on the telephone, I emailed him again saying: 'I played today like I didn't have a care in the world!'

I went on to have the summer of my life and I thank this man for connecting me back to what I had before, and more. I pitched against some of the best in the world at the Big League World Series. In 21 innings of pitching I had a 0.00 ERA.

Because of the good doctor's help, I am following my dream. I want more out of myself and my future. It has given me the confidence to believe in myself and my heart to get there. If you have lost it, there is hope." ---Ernie Herring

EXCITED BY THE CHALLENGE OF A DIFFICULT OPPONENT

Kaila Holtz pitched softball in the 2004 Olympics for Team Canada. An assistant coach at the University of Massachusetts she was at her wits end also wrestling her demons on the mound. She summarized her problem and the solution that occurred after we worked together:

"Something was holding me back from reaching my full potential. I would work and work to get myself into a position where the ball was in my hand for the game we needed to win and then something would happen. I would become unsure of myself and inevitably I would perform horribly. It felt like all my effort would uncontrollably come crashing down around me.

I tried to tackle my anxiety with the numerous strategies I have learned by being a sports psych nut. But nothing worked. Every variation of my pre-game routine or relaxation technique moved me farther away from the mental clarity I was seeking.

Ultimately, before I needed to pitch, I would end up with an inner battle between my rational thoughts and my anxious self. This discussion never ended well.

Together "The Doc" and I peeled back layers of my anxious inner demon. I am beginning to trust myself more in tough situations and I am excited by the challenge of a difficult opponent.

My pitching mechanics have also improved. I am more willing to play with spins and grips; I am throwing pitches I never had the courage to try before.

While working on my fear of the unknown in softball, other areas of my life have also shifted. I look at my watch less. I am more friendly to people I don't know. My eyes for life are brighter and I have stopped defining myself as a person by how well I perform on the mound.

Thanks Doc, for showing me why I love to pitch, making the game fun, and most importantly, enabling me to bring my best self to the ballpark every day.
--- Kaila Holtz

CHAPTER TWENTY-SIX

THE DISCONNECT WITH FIELDING

"Between the idea and the reality, between the motion and the act, falls the Shadow." --- T.S. Eliot

Committing errors is part of the game. Committing a number of errors in a brief period of time is a clear signal to intervene with a new course of action, rather than condemnation.

Darnell Coles, former Detroit Tigers' infielder, had no idea what hit him. There weren't many third basemen who ever struggled as severely as he did with the "little man" sitting on his shoulder. Coles pondered his meltdown with the Tigers that began in 1987:

> *"I went in knowing third base was mine. I was confident. The first six games of the regular season, I had three errors. Then disaster really struck. I had a three-error game in Kansas City, then a few weeks later I had three more in another game. It got to the point where I wanted to cry. I really didn't want the ball hit to me. I wanted to die. Just crawl in a hole."*

How do you explain the paradox of good ball players suddenly committing a high percentages of errors? By midseason 2004 when the Detroit Tigers led the majors in errors, then-Manager Alan Trammell was befuddled: "We do a lot of things that make me scratch my head. Just overall, we do some careless things that have cost us. As long as I'm involved in baseball, it will bother me. The question is: How can I fix it?"

By the sixth week into the 2004 season, former Los Angeles Angels utilityman Shane Halter was being stalked by his invisible opponent in the field, big time. The original point of its entry occurred during a crucial eighth-inning error against the New York Yankees. Halter committed a total of five errors in fours starts.

While manager Mike Scioscia said, "I don't think it's in his head," Halter had his own explanation: "It's like hitting. You get into a rut where you don't feel good. You second-guess every hop. When you're not feeling good, you need to be more aggressive. Right now, I'm more passive."

I MADE ALL MY PLAYS IN THE FIELD

Wayne MacKay's struggles at shortstop matched Darnell Coles' frustration back in the late '80's:

"I am the starting shortstop here at Saint Anselm College in New Hampshire. I won the job in the fall by my strong defensive play and ability to make contact at the plate and get on base. I worked real hard all fall and winter on my defensive play to improve my game and become the shortstop I want to be.

Last week we went down to Florida to begin our season and we played 11 games. I started the first five games and made about seven errors. I then got benched for three games because of my inconsistency.

I was given another chance the last three games and impressive with the bat, but the errors kept on coming. I don't know why all of a sudden I can't field a grounder when I was improving daily over the last year. I ended the trip with 11 errors in 28 plays and I don't know what to do.

I have lost a lot of my confidence and need it back to get back to my aggressive reckless abandon I usually possess while manning shortstop. I hope you can

135

give me some advice to get me through this and get me ready for the rest of the season.

I still have the spot now, but if things don't change it won't be mine for long. Help me!!!!!!!!!"

Wayne included a list of issues that kept him from performing:
- · I am becoming own worst enemy
- · My arm becomes stiff and robotic
- · I'm self-doubting and second-guessing myself
- · I'm worried about throwing the ball away
- · I'm overthinking
- · I'm having a self-confidence problem
- · I'm unable to turn off negative thoughts
- · I have a fear of failure

After one session Wayne emailed me his exciting results:

"We had all of our Friday and Saturday games cancelled because of the snow, but we did play Sunday in Pennsylvania. It was the worst playing conditions I have ever played in with winds and 25 degree temperatures and snow showers during both games of the doubleheader.

I played real well with probably my best two games so far this season. The first game I had eight plays to me in the field and I made them all. I felt real comfortable in the field despite the conditions. I went 2-for-3 with the bat and continued to stay hot at the plate.

The second game I only had two plays in the field, but made them both and again went 2-for-3 at the plate. I felt awesome in the field. I raised my batting average from .364 to .429.

It was a great feeling to have after the game knowing I made all my plays in the field. Thank you so much." --- Wayne MacKay

CHAPTER TWENTY-SEVEN

THE DISCONNECT IN
THE INFIELD

"I'll beat it. I know what I'm capable of doing. I know how good I can be. I know I'm an All-Star player. Its not like I'm trying to go somewhere I've never been. I'm trying to get back to what I've been." --- Chuck Knoblauch

Throwing errors do not necessarily occur on difficult plays, but commonly on easy ones. Rich McGinnis's invisible opponent presented itself in a likewise manner. He describes its point of entry:

"The first game of my junior year I air-mailed the first baseman a one-hop screamer from third. I had all the time in the world, but overthrew the first baseman very poorly. From that point on, I would struggle all year over simple throws from third base." --- Rich McGinnis

Former Los Angels Dodgers second baseman Steve Sax had a similar experience at the beginning of the 1983 season playing against the Montreal Expos while fielding a cut-off throw during Andre Dawson's triple. Dawson held on third, but then scored after Sax winged it home and it bounced away.

"It was a pretty average error. But I started thinking about it," said Sax. *"I started losing my confidence, my timing. Pretty soon they were gone."*

Sax's disconnect occurred at that exact moment in time of his errant throw to home. That error was the point of entry for Sax's invisible opponent to manifest in his wild mechanics.

Sax's invisible opponent nailed him for 30 errors that season until he met and conquered it later that August with one session. He did not commit another error the remainder of the year.

The disconnect of subsequent players struggling with such easy throws were called the "Steve Sax disease" and their errant tosses were labeled "Sax attacks."

A LIVING HELL ENDED

Nathan Emrick, a second baseman, became separated from his confidence and natural ability to throw to first base while playing at Southern Illinois University. I initially received two emails from Head Coach Dan Callahan:

"I am presently coaching a young man who is going through absolute hell right now because he cannot throw the ball to first base. Ironically, the only person who knows what he's going through is ME! What I went through personally, changed my life and it was a living hell for me.

Not to get too much into my history, but I went through this throwing phobia in college as a pitcher at the University of New Orleans in the mid-70's. I hit a kid with a pitch and all hell broke loose and the "thing" preoccupied two and a half years of my life. I later read about Steve Blass, Kevin Saucier, and later on some others, Wohlers, Knoblauch, Sasser, etc.

The young man I'm referring to was first-team all-conference last year and our team's MVP. He's a very good player and he has even received some pro interest.

This weekend at Stetson University in Florida, he made three throwing errors on routine plays. He has no feel; he's scared; and he's anxious. I could go on and on. This started in practice a couple weeks ago for some unexplained reason. It just appeared out of nowhere. We need to get him back where he belongs.

I don't know what to do, other than some drills that "might" work. He needs help and I guess I need help. He is miserable because he cares so much. Hopefully you/we can do something to help this young man, and ultimately our team. Any suggestions? Thank you for listening and I look forward to hearing from you." --- Coach Dan Callahan

Later that day I heard from Nathan:

"I have recently developed a problem throwing to the first baseman from my position at second base. It seems that I have no feel or touch for the baseball whatsoever anymore. It seems like a foreign object, not something I have been playing with for years.

For the first time in my baseball life, I was moved from a position because I just could not get the job done. I felt embarrassed and also that I let down my team.

Since I started playing baseball I always had a good arm, my only problem was that at times I could be inconsistent. During my college career I have played multiple positions, and always kind of used that as an excuse for my inconsistent throws. But now that I am playing one position, I have no excuse. I just cannot do what has always been so natural to me, and it is scary as hell. I don't know what to do. Hopefully you will."

I worked with Nathan on the issues he presented and later that same day received this email:

"After talking to you today, I went and worked out with my coaches. Today was a huge step in the right direction for me, I was able to take ground balls and I had no worries about throwing the ball away.

I was much more fluid and threw with more velocity than I have in a long time. I was not perfect today, but after throwing a ball away, I still had the confidence that I was going to make a great throw the next ground ball, and that was the biggest difference.

I took ground balls and threw with confidence no matter what happened on the previous ball. It was amazing, I think talking to you a couple more times will allow me to get over this "virus" and allow me to get back to the old me. I look forward to talking with you again and deeply appreciate what you have already done in just one session."

That same day I received a telephone message from Coach Callahan regarding his observations of Nathan in practice immediately after I worked with him:

"I saw progress without question. Nate had more bounce in his step. He looked more confident and felt better about himself. Compared to Saturday and Sunday, Monday was unbelievable. The difference was like night and day."

Two days later we worked on Nathan's release point and I received another update from Coach Callahan:

"Yesterday, Nathan and another middle IF split three buckets of balls, and I would estimate he took 70 ground balls. He threw one away. His confidence is great.

This weekend will obviously be a test, but I'm confident he is up for it. Maybe for old time's sake, I can bounce a couple balls off the backstop during BP! I wish I'd known you when I was in college. Thanks again." --- Coach Dan Callahan

Nathan emailed me 10 days later:

"This weekend at Ole Miss went better. I had better pre-game sessions and on Sunday I took ground balls for about 30 minutes and did not throw one ball away. Things are definitely looking up."

And then I heard from Nathan again a week later:

"This weekend went well defensively. I had one throwing error on a double play, but I actually threw it instead of lobbing the ball to first. I made about seven or eight plays that I made great throws on so I am definitely feeling better and better everyday."

The last communication from Nathan summarized how well he was doing:

"This weekend went really well. I am really starting to swing the bat better and am feeling more and more confident everyday. I can see that I am finally starting to get that swagger back that I had all last year. Thanks." --- Nathan Emrick

CHAPTER TWENTY-EIGHT

THE DISCONNECT
IN THE OUTFIELD

"Whatever you bury, you bury alive." --- Anonymous

By the end of May 2004 Toronto Blue Jays' Alexis Rios, a better-than-average outfielder, was struggling with tracking fly balls since being called up. Manager Carlos Tosca commented on Rios' perplexing performance:

> *"A couple of balls he broke in on, and we're going to take him out when we get on the road. His fly-ball footwork is something that we worked on the whole time he was there in spring training, and it's not happening for him right now. It's something that we're going to have to attack. Right now his footwork is lacking out there."*

The *something* "to attack" and completely destroy is Rios' invisible opponent that has been playing cat and mouse with him since spring training.

Imagine observing "the you" who is struggling and seeing that there is something else operating simultaneously creating your mechanical inconsistencies. By making the invisible visible, you too can obliterate your invisible opponent. From its ashes will emerge your personal symbolic phoenix. And your game is back.

IT'S WEIRD HOW QUICKLY IT WENT AWAY

Bill Rankin, a college outfielder, was being manipulated by his invisible opponent. Enough was enough so he contacted me:

"I'm a sophomore playing outfield at a Division One program. I found your website online a couple of days ago because I just started having trouble throwing again.

Since sophomore year in high school I've been having encounters with this throwing problem. It comes randomly, and relatively infrequently...but when it hits, it hits hard.

We just started fall practice and all of a sudden I can't even warm-up without throwing the ball over my partner's head or right into his spikes. When I go to release the ball, I feel completely disconnected from it...like I forgot how to throw. I'm a leader on the team and it's just so frustrating and embarrassing to not be able to make the simplest throws.

When I've battled this problem in the past it's always taken a little while...a week or two. Every time I beat it, I tell myself to never let it come back, but here it is again. Suddenly, one day I'll get the feel of the ball back and it's gone.

I'm just tired of spending those 10 days on a downward spiral of confidence and even losing sleep over it. I've spent entire days of school and classes thinking and worrying if I'll be able to warm-up that day at practice.

If you could help me, it would make my life so much easier right now! I'm tired of spending my day thinking about throwing a baseball, and I'm sick of telling my coaches I've got a sore arm."

We focused on his overthinking, frustration and how *something* was locking his wrist and affecting his release point. It interfered with his completely feeling the ball rolling off his fingertips. In a follow-up the next week Bill reported in:

"Your process was a totally different way of going after my problems. I feel fine. Everything went well. I'm not having any problems right now. My wrist's locking was gone the very next day! And I'm no longer thinking about my throwing during the day or while playing anymore. It's weird how quickly it went away."

Bill fired another email to me later and gave me the following update:

"Summer ball went fine. Our team won the regular season, but we lost our first game in the tournament so we had to battle out of the loser's bracket. We reached the finals, but lost four-to-one in the first game. Personally, I played well all season long...starting every game in center field and hitting in the two hole." ---Bill Rankin

Ken McLeod describes what I call the invisible opponent as *"a web of patterns that comprise the basis for our habituated reactions to situations. As we become aware of these patterns through our attention, it feels as if there is a person inside us who is operating independently of our intention and contrary to...our efforts to wake up and be present."* McLeod refers to this uncooperative "person inside" as the "appropriate opponent." You need to focus your attention on *it* as your adversary, and not on yourself.

I FEEL FREE AND ALIVE PLAYING BASEBALL

Justin Lepore, an outfielder in his junior year, found how easy it was to remove years of anxiety while playing in games by focusing on his invisible opponent and not himself:

"I am going to start to see a psychologist next week, but would like your input before. I am a Division One athlete at Marist College and would like to finally end my throwing block with your help.

The problem started my sophomore year in high school when I was catching and then sort of went away, but the throwing block was always in the back of

144

my mind. I stopped catching because I couldn't throw the ball back to the pitcher and moved to the outfield where I felt more comfortable because essentially, a bad throw from the outfield isn't as costly.

I received a baseball scholarship to Clemson University and the problem came up again when we were doing outfield drills that were short throws. I felt as though I was pushing the ball and sailing it over 10 feet, or under-throwing it 10 feet to the cut off man.

Anyway, I had elbow pain but continued to play through the whole fall and opted to red shirt in the spring to get Tommy John surgery by Dr. Andrews. After the spring, I transferred to Marist College, but even after the surgery, the problem still persisted.

This past summer, I played in the NECBL where I made All-League and played in the All-Star game as the DH (315 avg./ .500 slg.). I also played in the field for a few games and hit my cut off man every time, but the problem is anxiety.

I still always doubt myself that the problem with come back one day, which provides discomfort in other areas of my game. It's like I just cant relax and have fun because I am constantly thinking of throwing. I get this anxiety feeling in my chest and even though I feel as though my throwing problem has somewhat gone away, I just don't feel natural throwing a baseball and constantly doubt myself due to the fear it will come back."

We worked on Justin's anxiety for an hour and his next email tells it all:

"I am pretty amazed how your techniques worked. The anxiety I felt prior to our conversation is currently gone. I still feel a little nervousness though, which is normal, but not any anxiety.

I feel as though I am back to how I want to play the game of baseball; confident and trusting of my abilities. I am glad I took the time to call you because I feel the techniques you showed me can help me in other areas of my life that I take pride in.

I am still amazed at how my anxiety went away though. Scientists spend millions of dollars in medicine trying to find a magic pill to rid anxiety, but all I had to do was talk to you for an hour on the telephone. It's almost as though I feel free and alive playing baseball. Thank you." --- Justin Lepore

CHAPTER TWENTY-NINE

THE DISCONNECT
FOLLOWING SURGERY

"There is no reality except the one contained within us; that is why so many people live such an unreal life. They take the images outside them for reality and never allow the world within to assert itself." --- Herman Hesse

A player may have a medical procedure, such as Tommy John surgery, and is unable to play for the better part of a year. After fully recuperated and deemed physically fit, sometimes "something" keeps the player from returning to his or her pre-surgical level of performance.

Maybe when they heard they needed the surgery they feared they would never play again. Who knows? You don't have to know in order to help them. Whatever it was, something still has them disconnected from what they are capable of doing long after the date of their expected return.

As a result too many players recover physically, but whatever entered their psyche some time ago is still operating like a microchip sending out signals of bodily tension to alert them they are not out of the woods yet.

Chuck Shirley experienced it: *"I had Tommy John surgery when I was in high school and despite making one of the best and fastest recoveries, I have never been the same throwing the ball."*

I ENJOY BEING ON THE MOUND AGAIN

Adam Pallone, a pitcher from Central Connecticut State University, like Chuck Shirley, was never the same following surgery:

"Four years ago I was a very successful Division I college pitcher. Then I underwent Tommy John surgery and I have never been the same since.

The season after my surgery I was progressing as planned with my rehabilitation to the point where I was able to begin throwing live during my University's fall scrimmages. At this point I began to develop a difficulty throwing a pick-off to second base. This then turned into a problem picking-off at first base as well. And eventually I would either throw a ball in the dirt or way off-line to first when fielding a bunt or a come-backer.

I also started developing some shoulder pain at that time and eventually underwent a debridement procedure to clean-up my labrium in my throwing shoulder.

I then progressed in my rehab back to the point where I could begin pitching again, and that's when my throwing difficulties appeared again. I was always a pitcher who lived on control and location of my pitches. And I was always regarded as an excellent fielding pitcher as well, until the last few years.

I still love pitching and am currently working out to get ready for the start of next season. I've had no problems when I'm throwing to either a screen or just a catcher. But given my past problems in game situations, I was curious about any suggestions you might have about what I could do to prepare myself mentally for those situations. I look forward to any insight you might have."

I requested additional information from Adam:

Emailed September 30:

"The Ortho's and coaches that I have worked with believe my control problems on the mound are a result of faulty mechanics. I have worked with a pitching coach and the surgeon who performed my Tommy John reconstruction in my hometown of Syracuse, New York last season. I am lucky enough to have a surgeon who has worked in conjunction with my pitching coach and me to review slow-motion video tapes of my pitching.

The video tape helped me to focus on my tendency to rush thru my delivery which was resulting in my shoulder and elbow being "slow" thru the zone and placing a lot of unnecessary stress on my elbow and anterior shoulder. I've worked hard over the past year to correct that problem.

As far as my problem with throwing fielded groundballs accurately to a base, the only explanation any of my coaches or doctors have been able to give me is that "it's all in my head." At my pitching coaches suggestion I have been taking a lot of PFP's (pitcher fielding practice) with either throwing to a screen or to a teammate and have been able to do so without any problems. But it seems as soon as I get into a game situation or a scrimmage my problems resurface almost immediately."

On October 25, I worked with Adam on several issues: his initial warm up pitch usually going into the backstop or up and in; problem fielding balls off the mound; body tension; never getting the velocity back after having Tommy John surgery; pressure to be a leader, and pitching well in practice but not in scrimmages or actual games. He replied in several emails:

Emailed November 1:

"So far everything's been great. I threw a bullpen on Tuesday and then against some live hitters in a mini-simulation on Thursday, and both days felt great. My control was good and it felt like I was throwing a little harder then I have in the past year or so. I didn't really get an opportunity to field any groundballs or attempt to throw to first or get a chance to try any pick-offs (two of the things that have troubled me in the past).

But this upcoming Thursday I have an Alumni game for my college that I'm scheduled to pitch in. I'll drop you another email after that game with anything that I have noticed."

Emailed November 11:
"Last Thursday's alumni-game went great. I threw two innings with command and control of my pitches that I haven't been able to have in a long while: three strikeouts, no walks, and only one hit allowed. My velocity seemed like it was up a little from the last few times I've thrown bullpens too.

Everything felt unbelievably good while I was on the mound. It's a feeling that I haven't experienced in some time! I felt relaxed and confident; and I didn't feel like I had a strangle-hold on the ball like I used to sometimes. It was basically nice to be able to turn and throw to first and not have my mind "panic" and wind up two-hopping the ball over there.

I wanted to thank you again. It's hard to explain how difficult it was for me to almost be too "scared" of what might happen to pitch. You've allowed me to get back on the mound and enjoy being out there again." --- Adam Pallone

CHAPTER THIRTY

THE DISCONNECT FOLLOWING
AN INJURY

"The experience of transformation is therefore a kind of remembering; a remembering of our true condition, which we have forgotten." --- Michael Greenwall and Peter Nunn

Former New York Mets catcher Mackey Sasser's disconnect occurred in 1987 at the very moment a ball hit his shoulder during a Triple-A game in Calgary. Although he recovered from that injury he was never the same. He commented, *"Ever since then, I can't flick the ball back to the pitcher."* It got worse each year until Sasser lost his position, and his career.

Like Steve Blass, Mackey Sasser became the subject of an unwanted ironic tribute: the ever-mutating Sasser D computer virus was named after him.

At the beginning of the 2003 season, former Los Angles Dodgers first baseman/outfielder Shawn Green sustained a shoulder injury. He found himself in a prolonged slump the remainder of 2003 and halfway through the 2004 season.

Green knew it was more than simply his mechanics. They had been addressed over and over and over. He knew the problem. It was his missing the *feel* of being locked in at the plate.

On June 24, 2004 Green's chronic conflict with his invisible opponent reached a crescendo. Tony Jackson's article, "Frustrated Green Benched," in the *Daily News* captured it:

> *"Dodgers first baseman Shawn Green was benched Wednesday night, a concession to the fact he had killed several rallies in the previous two games and has struggled all season offensively.*
>
> *Both [hitting coach Tim] Wallach and Green declined to identify [his mechanical problem], but Green did say it had something to do with his hands.*
>
> *'It's something I have been working on, trying to get a feel,' [Green] said. That Green's mechanical flaw remains despite having been pointed out to him previously might be an indication that he hasn't been particularly receptive to outside input. 'He's receptive to anything you say to him,' [manager Jim] Tracy said. 'But he is a very intelligent guy, and he knows hitting.'"*

The following day, Los Angeles Dodgers catcher Paul Lo Duca commented how Green had worked tirelessly through a disappointing first half: *"The whole thing that blows my mind is that people think he's trying to hit the way he's hitting. No. He's just going through something right now. Whether it's mechanical or mental, you just don't know, but he cares. It's just a tough game for him right now."*

After reading these stories I communicated with Green. By noontime July 1, we were working together using his imagination to resolve his struggles at the plate.

Less than nine hours later, I was thrilled to watch Shawn break out of his prolonged slump by hitting a home run and a game-winning double against the Giants.

Green caught hold of his passion and reconnected with his natural *feel* at the plate again. The next morning Rich Hammond reported that breakthrough game for Green in the *Daily News* article entitled "Clutch hits twice as nice for Green:"

> *"The Dodgers rallied from a two-run deficit in the late innings, against one of the best pitchers in the game, and Shawn Green provided not one, but two, huge hits Thursday night. No joking.*
>
> *The Dodgers rallied from three different deficits and Green, who has received much of the blame for the Dodgers' offensive problems, had his best game in more than a month.*
>
> *[Green] came to bat in the seventh inning with the Dodgers trailing 4-2 against the Giants and 10-game winner Jason Schmidt.*
>
> *Schmidt threw a fastball on the first pitch, and Green belted it over the left-field wall for [a] home run.*
>
> *An inning later, Green got to be the hero against reliever Felix Rodriguez. Milton Bradley walked with one out, and Green hit a double in the left-center gap to drive in the go-ahead run."*

Green's teammates were happy to see him break out. *"It's just a matter of time for Shawn,"* said Paul Lo Duca, who also homered. *"He's our guy. If he gets hot, we're going to go."* Dave Roberts joined in the excitement and said, *"He looked great, swinging with a purpose and with confidence and he came up with a hit that was huge for the team and for Shawn."*

On July 16, Green had another positive experience, collecting three hits and driving in a run. And that was the night after hitting a two-out, go-ahead grand slam in the eighth inning as the Dodgers rallied for a 4-3 victory over Arizona.

By July 20, he was on fire and the press couldn't make heads or tails how such a transition occurred. Green's solo home run in the eighth inning provided the difference in a 7-6 victory over Houston. It appeared in Tony Jackson's *Daily News* article the next day:

> *"A little more than a month ago, slumping Dodgers first baseman Shawn Green said he hadn't felt truly locked in at the plate since 2002. Two nights ago, the suddenly-sizzling Green said he thought he was finally reaching that comfort zone that he hadn't experienced in two years.*
>
> *The results back him up. After batting .253 the first half of the season, Green entered Tuesday's game with Houston batting .389 (7 for 18) for the second half, with two homers, a double and seven RBI through the first five games.*
>
> *The reason for the sudden resurgence isn't readily apparent. But there are several possibilities, not the least of which is that Green had three days to clear his head over the recent All-Star break.*
>
> *It also could have something to do with mechanical adjustments, although hitting coach Time Wallach said Green hasn't made any major ones. It also could have to do with where Green is hitting in the lineup, although manager Jim Tracy has tried him third, fifth and sixth since taking Green out of the cleanup spot on June 24. Tracy discounts the lineup theory."*

By June 30, Green was batting .251 with nine home runs. July 1 was his turning point. Using his imagination, he was able to easily restore his original mechanics. Shawn and I worked together throughout the remainder of the season. He added 19 more homers and finished with a total of 28 -- not including three during the playoffs. He finished the remainder of the season batting .282.

He was then traded to the Arizona Diamondbacks where he ended the 2005 season hitting .286. His 22 home runs with the Diamondbacks brought his career total to 303.

THE END

OR RATHER JUST THE BEGINNING

After World War ll was over and Winston Churchill was no longer the prime minister of Great Britain, he was asked to give a commencement speech at his alma mater. It is presented here in its entirety without any editing or deletions. Churchill addressed the young graduates with advice how to deal with their futures:

"Never give up. Never. Never. Never."

APPENDIX A

SELF-ASSESSMENT SURVEY:
100 CHALLENGES PLAYERS CAN CONQUER

1. Inability to feel the release point ____
2. Inconsistent release point ____
3. Death grip on the ball ____
4. Releasing ball too late or too soon ____
5. Unable to respond to coach's expert advice____
6. Increased practice doesn't improve game ____
7. Mechanical difficulties make no sense whatsoever____
8. Improvement at practice gets lost during a game ____
9. Everything tried so far doesn't work ____
10. Becoming own worst enemy____
11. Missing location ____
12. Command is off____
13. Negative attitude effects game____
14. Concerned about disappointing others ____
15. Pressured meeting expectations ____
16. Self-judging and criticizing ____
17. Frustration and anger with myself is causing problems_
18. Persistent throwing problems ____
19. Arm becomes stiff and robotic ____
20. Bothered by embarrassing or humiliating memory____
21. Self-doubting and second-guessing ____
22. Worried about throwing the ball away ____
23. Ball doesn't feel comfortable in hand ____
24. Tingling sensation in hand ____
25. Numb feeling in hand or arm ____
26. No fluidity throwing ____
27. No longer throwing hard and firm ____

28. After successful surgery something holds me back from throwing____
29. Problem focusing and concentrating ____
30. Overthinking ____
31. Anxiety ____
32. Something negative is always in the back of my mind__
33. Timing is off ____
34. Struggling on the mound or plate ____
35. Slumps____
36. Dead arm ____
37. Feel disconnected ____
38. Problem throwing bullets ____
39. Inconsistent____
40. Control issues ____
41. Pressured to be perfect ____
42. Play well in practice, tense during a game ____
43. Self-confidence issues ____
44. Forget hitting strategy once I am in the box ____
45. Throwing 10 feet in front of pitcher or 10 feet over his head____
46. No problem throwing from anywhere except one place, i.e., 2nd to 1st___
47. Down/Depressed ____
48. Guiding the ball____
49. Lobbing the ball____
50. Wanting to give up the game I love ____
51. Committing errors ____
52. Difficulty turning off negative thoughts____
53. Rushing the delivery ____
54. Fear of failure ____
55. Can't throw well if somebody is behind my target ____
56. Can't locate strike zone ____
57. "Forgotten" stance ____
58. Whipping action problem in wrist/arm. ____
59. "Forgotten" how to throw ____
60. Lost feel for delivery ____
61. Lost feel for hitting ____

62. Velocity decrease for no reason ____
63. Problem throwing pick-off ____
64. Loss of accuracy ____
65. Two-hopping or three-hopping the ball. ____
66. Not having fun anymore ____
67. Problem when someone stands behind the person I am throwing to ____
68. Error-prone ____
69. Hard on myself ____
70. Fielding errors ____
71. Not locked in ____
72. Wrist locks when throwing ____
73. Can't buy a hit ____
74. Chasing pitcher ____
75. Giving up on myself ____
76. Bend in elbow____
77. Fear of success ____
78. Clutch situations ____
79. Negative attitude ____
80. Nervous batting in the box ____
81. Nervous when people are watching ____
82. Can't throw short distances or toss lightly without throwing ball away____
83. Double pumping ____
84. Throwing into the dirt ____
85. Throwing out of player's reach ____
86. Missing my spots ____
87. Holding onto the ball too long ____
88. Hitter's anxiety ____
89. Mechanics/velocity never same since surgery/injury ____
90. Rushing through delivery ____
91. Loose feel of ball off fingers ____
92. Forced delivery ____
93. Arm locks ____
94. Battling myself ____
95. When scouts/colleges/teams were interested, problem began ____

96. Problem throwing around the horn ____
97. Arm is not connected to my brain ____
98. Analyzing and agonizing more ____
99. Tense shoulders when nervous ____
100. Problem persists in light of sports psychology techniques of motivation, visualization, reviewing video tapes, etc. ____

APPENDIX B

This section contains the complete stories of the three ball players from chapter one: Ryan Johannes, Rich McGinnis and Blake Miller.

WHEN YOU AGONIZE YOU ANALYZE

The last thing you want is your mind overloaded with analysis and clutter. Ryan Johannes, a sophomore and first baseman from Pierce College in Washington, contacted me with this very problem:

"I have been playing baseball ever since I can remember. It's always been my best sport. Just over the past year or so I've starting experiencing throwing problems.

My parents and I traced this back to an event that occurred my senior season in high school when I made a bad throw back to the pitcher and a runner on third scored on the play while our third baseman was injured trying to slide and back up the throw.

Ever since that play I always lobbed the ball back to the pitcher and have never tried to throw it. The problem throwing persisted and started happening on all throws. I would take infield and not make one accurate throw.

I became very nervous to take infield before a game because the fans and other players would wonder what was going wrong with me. Because of this I didn't play much 1st base my freshman year at college and considered quitting baseball.

It got in the way of other parts of my game – it was something I was always worrying about.

I want to get rid of this problem completely so I can start having fun and enjoying baseball like I always have."

I consulted with Ryan over the telephone for less than two hours focusing on his throwing to the pitcher, worrying that prior problems might reappear, over-thinking, tension with close distance throws and general nervousness with certain aspects of his game. After the first session Ryan emailed me his results:

"I have been throwing very well lately. After our talk on Friday I threw fine in practice, which wasn't a surprise because I had already been doing that.

But on Saturday we had a double-header and I had been doing well enough in practice that I was starting at 1st base. I was quite nervous before the game, and worrying that in infield I would go back to throwing wildly and making a scene like I had experienced before.

Out of the first two throws I made to the catcher, one was over his head and one in the dirt. I started to panic a little and thought the problem was coming back.

But then somehow I was able to clear my mind and think about the images we had talked about that were there to help me and I loosened up and made a perfect throw into the catcher. After that, everything clicked and the rest of my throws in infield were perfect.

This is an accomplishment because I haven't taken a successful pre-game infield like that ever since I've been dealing with this problem in high school.

In the game I had to make one throw and it was absolutely perfect. There was a base-hit to center and the runner was trying to score from second. The center fielder hit me right in front of second base and I turned and relayed a perfect throw right to the catcher to beat the runner at the plate.

It surprised me that I was able to do that so easily. I just did it without even thinking -- which is good." --- **Ryan Johannes**

I OVERCAME THE MONSTER

My name is Rich McGinnis. I read your article on the sportsmaker web site regarding "Steve Blass Disease." I'm a 22 year old college student who has been battling the "monster" for the past five or six years.

I've lived with baseball's dark secret and tried to overcome it in every possible manner all the while trying to hide it from everyone around me. I felt embarrassed about having difficulty making a simple throw...one that anyone can do.

I first started having trouble my junior year of high school. I'd given up basketball so I could concentrate full time on baseball. I worked extremely hard all winter and had high expectations for the spring. I was a pitcher and a third base man. The first game of my junior year I air-mailed the first baseman a one-hop screamer to third. I had all the time in the world, but overthrew the first baseman very poorly.

From that point on, I would struggle all year over simple throws from third base. I also had a rough year pitching. I had shoulder problems unrelated to the monster that rendered me ineffective. I eventually lost my starting job at third and on the mound.

In the summer I started working out behind the plate. I'd caught when I was younger. I enjoyed a very good summer catching without any hints of the monster. However, early spring the monster would rear its ugly head again. I started having trouble throwing the ball back to the pitcher. I had no problems throwing to the bases or making quick snap throws, only when I had a lot of time.

I resembled Mackey Sasser when he would attempt throwing the ball back to the pitcher. I tried every conceivable mannerism to aid in my throw. I would pump two or three times; flop around behind the plate; crawl back and forth; and finally would walk out a few feet in front of the plate before lobbing the ball back.

After high school I tried out at college as a pitcher but didn't make it. My shoulder was still messed up and I opted to see an orthopedic. Two shoulder surgeries later I attempted to come back and pitch, but my arm wasn't where it should be. I began coaching my hometown's American Legion team. I really enjoyed coaching.

I hadn't seen the monster in two years, until this summer. I was throwing batting practice when all of a sudden I started having trouble. As we got deeper into the summer, I got worse. The monster was back.

I leaned on the sore arm crutch to avoid a compete meltdown. I never had trouble throwing strikes before. I was losing some of my passion for the game. People who have never experienced this don't understand. It's not as simple as 'Don't think. Just throw.' It's embarrassing. And it isn't nerves. I've been in some pressure-packed situations in baseball and have come through without a problem.

That's what makes this so frustrating and difficult. It's so simple and requires virtually no high degree of skill. When I'd go to throw, I'd feel totally unconnected with the ball. I couldn't feel the ball (if that makes sense). Before I had the problem, I could feel the ball right off the finger tips....it was like an extension of my arm. When I have trouble, it's like a foreign object. I was commonly told "You're your worst enemy. "

It was July 3, 2003 that I found Dr. Crowley's name online and decided to E-mail him. He contacted me and began to help me immediately with his unique method over the phone. Among topics discussed was a reoccurring dream I've had ever since I was about 12 years old. It was more frequent then, but I still have it from time to time as I gotten older. In the dream I'd be on the mound and would go to throw the ball, but I couldn't release the ball. I'd wake up feeling anxious, but would be quickly reassured that it was just a dream....until my junior year when my dream became a reality.

Within days after working with Dr. Crowley to overcome the monster, I became aware of a profound change in the dreams that had haunted me for years. I was actually throwing free and easy in my dreams. I can't remember ever having a dream in which I was doing that. The dream's entire landscape changed from a dark, tense background into a bright, relaxed atmosphere where I was throwing free and easy...and having fun. Once more baseball has become fun for me. And once again I'm excited about it!

When the problem had plagued me the worst, I didn't want to watch or even talk baseball once I left the field. However, after being helped by Dr. Crowley and his remarkable method, my passion for baseball has been renewed. I played catch shortly after our initial phone conversation and threw with ease.

While conquering this problem doesn't happen overnight, Dr. Crowley has put me back on the right track. I'm back to where I was before I had problems this summer. Until I worked with Dr. Crowley I was battling a monster that seemed unbeatable.

I know how it feels to try and hide baseball's dark secret and to deny even to yourself that you have a problem. I remember watching the 2000 NLCS and seeing Rick Ankiel struggle and melt down before a national audience. I remember my college friends laughing and making fun of him and I remember not thinking it was funny at all. I felt bad for him because I knew what it was like to battle the monster. It would have changed everything for Ankiel if they had let Dr. Crowley work with him.

If any player is battling with their own throwing monster, I strongly urge you to contact Dr. Crowley. Working with him was amazing and I believe his way of approaching the monster was extremely helpful . Dr. Crowley, once again, thanks for everything." --- Rich McGinnis

BACK ON TRACK

Blake Miller, a college pitcher, was struggling with the mental aspects of his game. Previous help provided information, but no solutions:

"I am a sophomore at Coker College. I've had trouble with my pitching for the last few years and have actively been looking for help for my mental problem. I have always been told that I do not pitch up to my potential and that it is due to

a mental problem.

The problem is that as helpful as my coaches are at pointing out problems, they have yet to give me any productive advice for how to fix it.

I'm not a professional prospect or even a top level college player. However, I would like to be able to pitch to my best abilities and have as successful a college career as I can.

I usually pitch well in the bullpen, but then I am unable to transfer it to the mound.

I have read books and consulted coaches, but have been unable to translate it into anything productive.

We worked several hours on Blake's forcing the action, being inconsistent, trying too hard, loss of control, loss of velocity, and anxiety on the mound. I received emails regarding his progress:

"We've already started fall practices and conditioning. I've been throwing bullpens about three days a week for the last two weeks and have been doing really well. I've had a little trouble with my change-up but I think it's due to trying to do a little too much with it. So I'm working on fixing that now."

Then Blake met another monster on his path that gave us further clues with which to focus:

"I need help! I threw really well through all of our bullpen sessions with the exception of little bit of control loss to my change-up, but when we started throwing to live hitters last week my first outing was terrible. We threw to hitters again today in an intra-squad practice and again it was terrible. A better word would probably be embarrassing.

Since we did the first live throwing session it seems like I have lost my mechanics. Even when throwing on the side all of my movements seem foreign. It also seems like I have no arm strength and am constantly throwing behind to hitters and are overmatched.

At one point over the summer I had gotten to where I could throw my change to any spot I wanted, but now I do good just to get it to the plate. I have also lost control over my other off-speed pitches.

Aside from all those I have also lost my confidence. I need help to get back on track."

We hooked up again and this time addressed Blake's trying too hard, lack of arm strength, overthrowing to compensate, feeling pressure, having to be perfect, embarrassment, problems with his change-up and self-doubts. He followed up with his progress reports:

"Well, I threw live to hitters today and I did pretty well...seventy-five percent strikes with a couple hits off of bad pitches. But that's what happens when you throw bad pitches. I still had a little trouble with my change-up, but I think it is getting better. I also made a small change in my mechanics and I think that it helped a lot with slowing myself down.

Overall I felt a lot more confident and composed and hopefully it will carry over into our scrimmage this weekend."

"We played our first fall game Saturday and I did pretty well. I faced three hitters and had three ground ball outs. I got behind in the count to every hitter, but I was able to throw strikes when I needed to so it was pretty good.

It's going good and I think I'm starting to get back on the right track. We have another game Friday night and then we'll have the next week off."

"Friday's game went well. I pitched one inning and threw 8 pitches. I'm still having trouble with my change-up though. Most of the comments that I get with that is that I am dragging my arm.

I'm starting to feel a lot more comfortable and confident on the mound now so I think I am finally heading in the right direction again.

On the mound now I only focus on the catcher's mitt. I can see an improvement myself."

We worked on his change-up again and doubts while releasing the ball. As a result Blake became aware of the feeling of doubt just as his foot went forward.

"We just got done with our fall workouts and after a few struggles in prior outings, I threw probably the best that I've thrown all year. I threw two innings and threw like 76% strikes with four strikeouts against some of the better hitters on the team with no walks and no runs.

I had command over all of my pitches and over myself. It felt great!

I was looking over my stats that my coach keeps when I got back to school the other day. Since I started working with you at the end of last year until now I have not given up an earned run in a live game or scrimmage against another team." --- Blake Miller

BIOGRAPHICAL SKETCH

Dr. Richard Crowley has worked in the field of human behavior for over thirty-five years. He pioneered and developed an innovation in sports enhancement called Mentalball, a unique approach that identifies and solves athlete's struggles whether they are mechanical or mental in nature.

Dr. Crowley holds a B.A. in psychology from St. Bonaventure University in New York, an M.S.W. in psychiatric social work from Boston College School of Social Work, a Ph.D. in clinical psychology from the United States International University in San Diego, and was awarded a National Institute of Health fellowship in community mental health. He served as a captain in the Army Medical Service Corps.

His professional training includes an internship and a fellowship at Harvard University's primary medical and psychiatric institutions. He has lectured abroad, appeared as a guest on countless radio and national television interviews including the Charlie Rose Show, the Merv Griffin Show and ESPN.

He has co-authored numerous articles and books with Dr. Joyce Mills including the award-winning, worldwide used text, *Therapeutic Metaphors for Children,* in print since 1986. It has been translated into Italian, French, German and Russian.

Dr. Crowley's work with professional athletes began with the former Los Angeles Dodgers rookie infielder Steve Sax in 1983 who was struggling to make routine throws to first base. Sax benefited from one session.

As a consultant to professional and amateur athletes in baseball, softball, archery, ultimate fighting, K-1 boxing, golf, darts, triathlon, equestrians, etc., his Mentalball approach has gained him international attention helping athletes to quickly overcome their struggles and enhance their performance. Examples can found on his website www.sportsmaker.com.

Dr. Crowley's methodology benefits a diverse audience that has expanded from athletes to the corporate world, sales and even stock brokers and day traders. He is frequently called upon as an invited speaker and workshop facilitator presenting the diverse applications of the Crowley Method and Mentalball.

Dr. Crowley is a member of the American Baseball Coaches Association, the advisory board of the On Deck Foundation at www.ondeckfoundation.org, and a lifetime member of the Association of Professional Baseball Players of America.